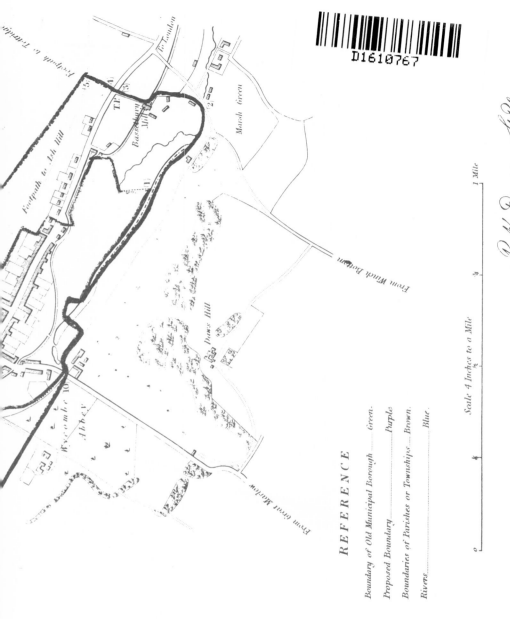

THE BOOK OF WYCOMBE

FRONT COVER: High Street, High Wycombe in 1772, from an engraving
by William Hannan.

ABOVE: Wickham from the Marlow Road, 1824. BELOW: High Wycombe
High Street, 1846, by E.J. Niemann.

THE BOOK OF WYCOMBE

BY
IVAN SPARKES

BARRACUDA BOOKS LIMITED
BUCKINGHAM, ENGLAND
MCMLXXIX

PUBLISHED BY BARRACUDA BOOKS LIMITED

BUCKINGHAM, ENGLAND

AND PRINTED BY

FRANK ROOK LIMITED

TOWER BRIDGE ROAD

LONDON SE1

BOUND BY

BOOKBINDERS OF LONDON LIMITED

LONDON N5

JACKET PRINTED BY

WHITE CRESCENT PRESS LIMITED

LUTON, ENGLAND

LITHOGRAPHY BY

SOUTH MIDLANDS LITHOPLATES LIMITED

LUTON, ENGLAND

DISPLAY TYPE SET IN

MONOTYPE BASKERVILLE SERIES 169

BY SOUTH BUCKS TYPESETTERS LIMITED

BEACONSFIELD, ENGLAND

TEXT SET IN 12/14PT BASKERVILLE

BY BRIAN ROBINSON

NORTH MARSTON, ENGLAND

© Ivan Sparkes 1979

ISBN 0 86023 062 7

Contents

Introduction and Acknowledgements

In writing this survey, I am aware how fortunate we are in the rich treasure of books, articles and photographs which have survived covering the history of Wycombe. This is largely due to the scholarship and interest of earlier historians. The work of L. J. Ashford and L. J. Mayes in producing the three volume history of the Borough in 1960 is remarkable for its authenticity and research, while the 19th century fact-collecting of Henry Kingston and John Parker created a tradition of interest in the civic traditions which has been evident ever since.

Contemporary sources, such as the pages of the *Bucks Free Press* are invaluable, and the articles they foster, for example the series by Francis Colmer in the 1930s, all add to our knowledge of the area. The historical collections at High Wycombe, Aylesbury and at the County Record Office are essential in interpreting the past fully, and we should thank past and present archivists, librarians, indexers and researchers for making this material available to local historians. Photography also brings the past alive, and the town is fortunate in the industry of J. P. Starling who established his studio in Frogmore in 1878, and in that of the Sweetlands, father and son, whose negatives, due to the generosity of Hamnett Raffety of High Wycombe, are preserved for the community.

I would particularly like to offer my thanks to those who have personally drawn my attention to historical materials, such as Miss T. E. Vernon, Mr R. Watts, Mrs M. Osers, and to Laurie Stevens who did much of the photography for me. Many still contribute to the story of Wycombe. David Woods has located many unusual and interesting documents, Ronald Goodearl has copied postcards and faded photographs for many years, adding greatly to visual documentation. The High Wycombe Society also has an important part to play in the preservation of buildings, a story told visually in the many drawings of Lorna Cassidy.

Even more essential has been the spirit of the town itself, which has survived changes and setbacks, and originated with a group of some twenty Burgesses in the 13th century, who founded an industrial town now the focus for a population of a hundred thousand, truly echoing the Borough motto: 'Industry Enriches'.

High Wycombe, 1979

Foreword

High Wycombe is without doubt the fastest developing residential and commercial centre in Bucks, and yet has by no means sacrificed its historic face, even if it has lost its cherished Borough status. It can point to a history as rich and diverse as any other town in the county. Since Ashford and Mayes' major work long since went out of print, Wycombe has lacked a modern record. *The Book of Wycombe* therefore fills a major gap in local bookshelves.

As a sometime Bucks journalist who has since attempted to chronicle other Bucks towns, I am aware of the considerable task Ivan Sparkes has faced. That he has succeeded in distilling the many and varied records to give a concise, factual yet fascinating account of the town's past is a tribute to his perception, persistence and penmanship, and a reflection of the dedication and concern typical of the county's library organisation of which he is part. Mr Sparkes is close to the records and knows what Wycombe people seek to know.

I regard it as a particular honour to be asked to write these few words of introduction, and I have no hesitation in commending the book to the people of the town, for it will enrich there understanding just as industry has enriched the town itself.

Radclive Hall, Buckingham

The Beech-clad Hills

The beech-clad hills of Bucks, which spontaneously adorn and beautify the Hundreds of Desborough, encompass not a more picturesque valley than it does the place where stands my Native Town.

Sequestered little spot! Adorned by nature with many delightful varieties of hill and dale, it seems to afford security for retirement; and those who love to watch the sparkling brook, and gaze with delight on the verdure and fertility of the surrounding pasture, in preference to luxury; or repose in the shade of the secluded woods, rather than seek the honours of princes, or the equinoctial hurricanes of political notoriety, may dwell for a time in Wycombe and 'babble o' green fields'.

Henry Kingston, 1848

ABOVE: Flint arrowheads found at Keep Hill, Barrow Croft Field, Wye Valley and Terriers, and flint axes found at Sands, Desborough Castle, High Wycombe and Toweridge, near West Wycombe. BELOW: A middle Bronze Age urn, one of three found at Barrow Croft, High Wycombe, in 1888.

Lands and Lords

'High Wycombe' states the *Victoria History of the County of Buckinghamshire,* 'is the first town in Buckinghamshire in point of size, and perhaps the most important from the point of antiquity and historic importance', and few of its older families would quarrel with that description. It lies centrally in a long valley, along which the River Wye flows down to the Thames. The western side is linked by the Bledlow and Saunderton Valley to the Upper Icknield Way which was probably one of the earliest and most important of the prehistoric routes in the Southern counties.

As the Ridgeway enters the boundaries of Bucks at Bledlow, it winds over the chalky heights to become the Upper Icknield Way, and at Bledlow is the gap in the escarpment which might well have attracted the ancient traveller to turn off the main route and follow the valley to the future site of High Wycombe. There was also a low ridgeway green walk which led round the west side of Lodge Hill to the ancient hill fort at West Wycombe. Archaeological evidence along this route indicates that it was in use from the Neolithic period.

New Stone Age men moved into the High Wycombe Valley about 2500 BC. They buried their dead in barrows, as in the kidney-shaped mound near the Icknield Way at Whiteleaf Cross. They also made rough pottery, and sherds of the Beaker People's pottery have been discovered beneath the Roman Villa site on The Rye in High Wycombe. Stone axes, some polished, have been found at Sands, Desborough Castle and High Wycombe, leaf-shaped flint arrowheads of the Neolithic period at Wheeler's Farm, Water End, while near Wycombe a prehistoric flint mine was discovered during construction of the railway in 1902. Here a much worn miner's pick made of deer antler was found next to the marks made in the chalk by the prehistoric workmen.

The invasion by the Beaker People during the 2nd century BC left its local mark with pottery and a burial group discovered in 1932 at Micklefield. This included a skeleton lying in a crouched position in an oval grave. In 1888 a plough horse's foot broke open a cavity in Barrow Croft Field at Wycombe Marsh, containing an important group of burial urns, the largest 19 inches high, the next about 7 inches high, while within the large urn was a cremation and an even smaller piece of pottery known as a pygmy cup. These items were dated as 1,000 BC and placed in the British Museum.

Flint arrowheads were still in use during the Bronze Age and have been located in and around High Wycombe, while bronze axes, more typical of the time, appeared at

Hazlemere and on the West Wycombe Road. With the Iron Age came hill forts, and just above the valley at Sands is the ancient Desborough Castle. This consists of a ring-work and traces of an earlier outer hill-fort, and in 1968, C. Saunders revealed a bank and ditch, probably of the Iron Age. Across the valley, now built over the church and churchyard of West Wycombe, was a large fortified Iron Age camp covering three acres and enclosed by a double circle of ramparts. Parts of the camp's inner vallum and ditch can be seen alongside the churchyard fence, and even today, as graves are dug, Iron Age 'A' pottery sherds are thrown up nearby.

Overlooking the Rye itself are the earthworks of Keep Hill: in 1826, two labourers split open a hollow flint which contained eleven British gold staters of Tasciovanus (minted at St Albans). More recently Iron Age 'A' sherds have been found there. On the other side of the valley adjoining the cemetery lies Malmer's Well. In 1863 'a pit was discovered, eight feet in diameter at the top, and slightly tapering to a diameter of six feet at the bottom' which was capped with dressed flints, and contained charred wood, burnt bones and several pieces of black pottery and other pieces of coloured pottery sherds.

In most instances, signs of occupation have been on the hills and slopes surrounding the Wye Valley, but in the 1st century AD there was a movement to the valley bottoms. About AD 70-90 the first Roman villas in the Chilterns were built at Hambleden, Saunderton, Latimer and High Wycombe.

The *Ledger Book* of 1722 refers to the High Wycombe Roman Villa when a mosaic floor was discovered by the workmen of the Abbey Estate.

The villa was established about AD 150-170 adjacent to a native farm already on the site. A boundary wall on the east side indicates that the whole was enclosed, and probably surrounded by a garden or orchard. The villa was a double corridor type with a central ridge roof ending at the two wings with clerestory windows to light the inner rooms of the central section. It was 104ft wide by 70ft deep, with walls of unknapped flints set in hard brown mortar. The floors were laid with red tile cubes, with the exception of the room with the mosaic, and the servants' quarters which were probably laid with rushes. A Roman lamp was found in London Road in 1952.

The most notable feature was the elaborate bath-house which consisted of a sequence of variously heated rooms. There was also an unheated room for undressing, out of which was built a half-round pool which acted as a cold plunge. All were floored with red tile cubes and the water supply was carried in wooden water pipes, the iron collars of which were found during excavation. The bathhouse was probably intended to serve the estate. Even more elaborate alterations were made in the 4th century, but it was abandoned following the collapse of the Roman Empire in the early 5th century. Weaving implements and spindle whorls have also been found. Other Roman links with High Wycombe are not well authenticated. In the garden next to the 'Priory' in Castle Street, High Wycombe a Roman well and a tesselated pavement were discovered c 1870, while part of a Roman jar was found in High Street, and a bronze furniture mount fashioned in the shape of a head on Keep Hill, in 1862.

Saxon settlements began about AD 600. The Saxons were not unversed in medical skill, as the skeleton of a man found at Bledlow Ridge had both arms broken in life and reset with skill. Another Saxon burial took place at Castle Hill, near the railway cutting at High Wycombe: a skeleton with iron weapons and a circular gold pendant around its neck. The pendant was of Kentish origin and of fine gold filigree. This house lies between two ancient ways which went northwards towards Terriers, known locally as the British Way or Hollow Lane. One went up by the side of the cemetery, almost parallel to Amersham Hill, and the other, starting by the Beaconsfield Arms in Hughenden Road, met it behind the Grammar School grounds at the back of Ridgeway. At the top of Brand's Hill Avenue, a collection of Romano-British pottery was found, and Brand's Hill House itself has been linked with Brand, son of Syve or Saegifu, who was sister to Suarting, a prominent local Saxon. Research has suggested that the pottery also identified the site of Brand's House with a possible residence or lodge of the Earls of Mercia.

Few records chart the history of Wycombe in the Saxon period, although the Chronicle of King Egbert's Conquests by Fabrius Ethelwerd informs us that 'on the very same day as Egbert was raised to the kingdom of the West Saxons, Ethelmund was passing through a farm, Wiecum, intending to go to a ford called Kempsford...' which John Parker calls Cumberford and dates the event as AD 800. Anglo-Saxon Wycombe was neither town nor borough, and in the time of Edward the Confessor was in the hands of the Saxon thane Brietric, who held it of Queen Edith with a value of £12. West Wycombe at this time was held by a freeman listed as a 'man of Archbishop Stigand'. These manors were part of the large estate known as the Honour of Wallingford, granted by King Harold. As Wigod allowed the Conqueror to cross the Thames at Wallingford on his march to London, he was allowed to keep his lands, and after his death c 1070, Robert D'Oilgi held them following his marriage to Wigod's daughter Aldith.

The Domesday book of 1086 records: 'Robert holds Wycombe himself from his wife's holding, it answers for 10 hides, land for 30 ploughs; in Lordship 4 hides, 3 ploughs there. 40 villagers with 8 smallholders have 27 ploughs. 8 slaves and 4 boors; 6 mills at 75s a year; meadow for 3 ploughs; for the horses of the court, and for the villagers ploughs, woodland 500 pigs. Total value £26; when acquired £10; before 1066 £12.' The manor of Wycombe consisted of some 2½ miles of valley, the hills on each side as far as the woodland and scrub for a mile or two. The Domesday population made this area one of the more heavily populated in the later county. The six mills, together with eight mills in adjacent Wooburn and three at West Wycombe, totalled seventeen along this stretch of the River Wye, an industry on which the commercial wealth of the town has flourished.

The population was spread in groups along the Wye, with hamlets at Bassetsbury, at Loakes (then Horsenden) and at the Church, which together were known as the 'Wicumbes'. When Wigod of Wallingford was forced to leave in 1068, he 'removed to the outberry of Wycombe' which could possibly be the village or hamlet of Bassetsbury.

Instead of large square fields, the nature of the valley caused them to be long and thin, so that West Field was three quarters of a mile long and only 250yds wide in parts. The Newland Meadows and the Townfield were still in mediaeval strips and identifiable areas up to the 19th century.

Westfield and Westfield Wood were still intact in 1763, as well as the lay to the west of Loakes Manor, taking up the site of the present Hospital, football ground and the recreation ground beyond it. Other fields mentioned about 1170 were Estfeld (East Field) and Middelfeld (Middlefield) and smaller fields called Tygelfurlong and Rubefurlong.

On the death of Robert D'Oilgi the manor of Wycombe passed to his daughter Maud who Henry I, as overlord, had married to Brian Fitzcourt. On Henry's death, Brian, holding the Castle of Wallingford, came out in support of Matilda in her fight against Stephen for the throne of England. When Matilda was defeated in 1141, Brian fled with her to Devizes 'showing that as before they had loved one another, so now neither adversity nor danger could sever them'. Stephen had besieged Brian Fitzcourt at Wallingford Castle and in 1152 he besieged him again at Wycombe. In 1153 he was brilliantly relieved by Henry of Anjou, and as proof of Stephen's presence at the seige there is a charter signed in 1153 'apud Wycumban in obsidione'. It is possible that the siege took place at the motte and bailey at Castle Hill. This is 30ft high and overlooked the church. The mound is made of layers of flints, rubble and thousands of horn cores of the mediaeval period. In 1820 parts of several large arrows were discovered in the grounds of Castle Hill House.

In due course the Honour of Wallingford (and Manor of High Wycombe) passed to Matilda's son, the future Henry II. He in turn granted 'the burg and foreign vill. of Wycombe' to Wigain of Wallingford, apparently a nephew of Brian Fitzcourt, and by 1171 Thomas Basset acquired a life grant. The Chronicler Matthew Paris makes special mention of Thomas Basset and Robert de Vipont as the King's evil councillors in 1211. In 1203 King John had divided the manor between Alan Basset and Ralph Vipont. Alan Basset and his brothers Gilbert and Thomas accompanied the King to Northampton when the King of Scots did homage in 1200. He accompanied the King to Ireland in 1210, and to Runnymede 15 June 1215, when his name, with that of his brother Thomas appeared on Magna Carta among those of the King's councillors. On his death he was succeeded by his son Gilbert (d 1241) who was created Baron of Wycombe. He lost the goodwill of Henry III and in August 1233 was outlawed and orders were given for the destruction of all towns, castles and parks belonging to him. On his death he was succeeded by his brother Fulk Basset, appointed Dean of York in 1239, who acquired the Basset estates in 1241 when he was also elected Bishop of London. Fulk Basset acted against the Pope in supporting the English clergy, and when Henry of Bath, the Justiciary, who had married into the Basset family, was accused of treachery, he also gave his aid. Henry III unwisely uttered the hasty wish 'If any one shall slay Henry of Bath he shall be quit of his Death', and was warned that Fulk Basset would exercise his spiritual powers against him while brother Thomas would impose his temporal strength. Fulk Basset stated 'The Pope and the King may indeed take away my bishopric for they are stronger than I; let them take away my mitre, and my helmet will remain'. When Fulk died in 1271 he was followed in his estates by Philip Basset the younger brother, who in July 1262 took charge of the kingdom in the King's absence abroad and presided over a parliament held in October 1262.

Philip Basset's estate went to his grandson Hugh le Despencer in 1281, but his influence at court was not to his advantage, for he was executed at Bristol in 1326, and his son was similarly executed in November 1326, his head fixed on London Bridge. In time the manor of Bassetsbury passed to Joan Countess of Hereford, mother-in-law of Henry IV, who possibly lived here as she took part in town events. After her time the castle fell into ruin; in 1420 it is mentioned as the 'old Castell' and a year earlier the residence was described as including a small hall with two adjoining rooms, a large tiled grange, a small grange, a cowshed with stable and 1½ acres of land. The land below the castle was wooded and known as Castle Green, and in 1411 Richard Sperlyng was prosecuted for cutting down the Lord's wood, while in 1417 John Frenchschmen was stated to have comitted trespass on Castle Green.

The manor was granted to the Dean and Canons of St. George's, Windsor in 1483, and was leased over the years to several families until 1717 when it was acquired by Sir Francis Dashwood.

When King John split the Manor of Wycombe in 1203 the other part went to Robert Vipont until he granted it to the Knights Templar in 1227 when it became known as Temple Wycombe, and later when the order of the Templars was suppressed, transferred to the Knights Hospitallers, who held it until the Dissolution. It went to the Raunce family in 1585 until it passed to Henry Petty, Lord Shelburne in 1700. The other manor of Loakes, was in 1482 in the hands of Robert Bardsey, and finally went to Richard Archdale about c 1605; he also had an interest in Temple Wycombe Manor, with which Loakes was thereafter identified. The present building, Wycombe Abbey, was built in 1795 on the site of the older manor house, in turn preceded by the ancient Hospital of St Margaret and St Giles.

In the time of Edward the Confessor West Wycombe was in the hands of Archbishop Stigand, and according to Domesday, had a large and flourishing milling and fisheries economy. It answered for '19 hides, land for 23 ploughs; 27 villagers with 8 smallholders, 19 plough, 7 slaves, there were 3 mills valued at 20s, and one fishery of 1,000 eels, meadowland for 7 ploughs and woodland with 1,000 pigs'.

In 1086 the manor was in the hands of the bishops of Winchester, and its rents and produce were held for the monks of Winchester until 1551 when Bishop Poynet surrendered it to the Crown, and in the next year it was leased to Sir Robert Dormer. In the 16th century, the young Princess Elizabeth stayed overnight with the Dormer family *en route* to the Tower of London. 'The Lady Elizabeth arrived here yesterday all dressed in white surrounded by a great company of the Queen's people. Her face was pale and stern; her look proud, lofty and distainful, by which she endeavoured to conceal her trouble.' In 1670 Charles, Earl of Carnarvon, transferred the estate to a London alderman, Thomas Lewis, husband of Elizabeth Dashwood. He became Member of Parliament for Wycombe, and in 1698 passed the estate to his brothers-in-law Samuel and Francis Dashwood, while in 1706 Francis obtained full ownership by payment of £15,000 to Samuel's son George, and for a token payment of 5s to Samuel's widow Anna.

Many of the quarrels in the past developed between the 'Borough' and the 'forrens' which were those parts of the Temple Wycombe and Bassetsbury manors outside the narrowly defined boundaries of the mediaeval borough. One such area was the Newlands, which took that name by 1227 when it was called *la Newlande,* for here, south of the river and following its course, was a belt of meadowland about 200yds wide and half a mile long which was used by, but not in the Borough. Beyond the scattered cottages in Frogmore were also the forrens; up Crendon Lane, past the gate which was closed at night were the same distant areas. The village of Crendon was mentioned as Croendena c 1220, and in 1421/2 'Le Manoir de Cronden' was valued at £24.

At about this time Thomas Hampden purchased lands in Wycombe forrens called Toterugge from William Clarke of Wycombe, while much earlier in 1179 it was called Tuterugge, or Tota's ridge or 'Look-out-Hill'. The lane leading to Totteridge was called Totridge lane by William Alleyn in 1517.

Other hamlets were Crendon Hatch and Haselemere, but Tarryers —or Terriers— was not mentioned until 1714. The other side of the valley was represented by The Creys in 1366 or The Cressche in 1368 which had become Cressicks by 1766, beyond which, now crowned by the Wycombe Sports Centre was 'Le Onhandedecruch' or the one handed cross, now known as Handy Cross. Along the ridge were Flacwelle in 1227 (Flackwell Heath), La Ludwatere in 1241 (Loudwater), the Dusteburg (1227) and Disborowe (1626) (Desborough Castle).

West Wycombe was itself Haveringedune (1222), then Haveringdon in West Wycombe (1241) while the name West Wicumbe appears in 1195. Such parts of the Borough as 'atte Reye' (1372) and 'The Reye' (1451) show the age of this meadowland, and the mills on the river included 'La Pande' (13th century), 'La Penmell' (1344) and 'Penn Mill' (1606), with 'Bughendune (c 1215) for Bowden Mill and 'Bassettysbury' in the 13th century.

The name of the area itself goes back to c 970 when 'Wicumun' was in use, varied over the years to 'Wicumbe' (1086), 'Wicumdena' (1157), 'Weycumbe' (1227); 'Wycombe Marchaunt' (1340), 'Chepingwycombe' (1478) and 'Cheaping Wycombe' with 'Magna Wykeham' (1545). The name probably comes from the River Wye with the second part of 'cumb' meaning valley, though there is an earlier possible spelling of 'Wichama' AD 799-802 the dwelling near the 'Wic' (dairy farm). The prefix of Chepping or Chipping means market. The Borough was called the Borough of Chepping Wycombe although the town itself was generally known as High Wycombe. The Chepping prefix continued officially as the name of the Borough until 1946.

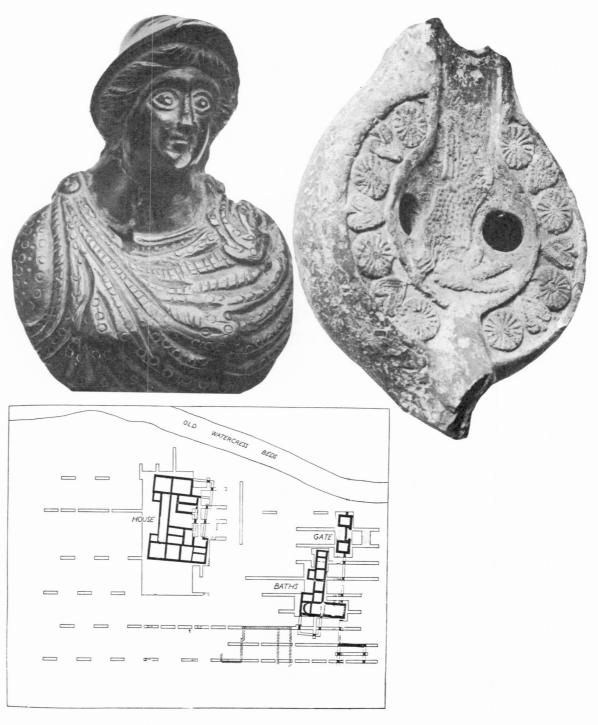

ABOVE LEFT: A Roman bronze furniture ornament found at Keep Hill in 1862. RIGHT: A Roman lamp found in London Road in 1952, and BELOW: a site plan of the Roman villa on the Rye.

ABOVE: Drawing of the Roman mosaic found in the villa, and BELOW: an
excavation of the site showing the mosaic in position.

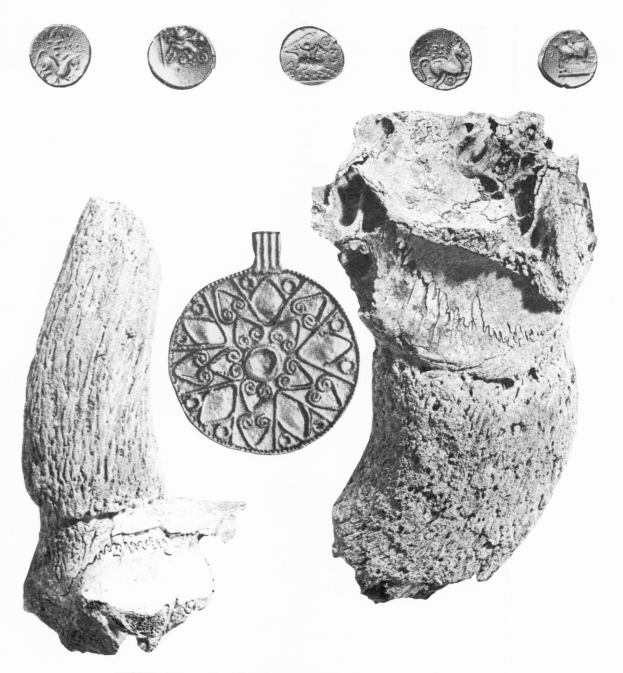

ABOVE: Five ancient British gold staters, found at Keep Hill, High Wycombe, in a hollow flint. CENTRE: An Anglo-Saxon gold pendant, probably of Kentish design, found at Keep Hill. BELOW: Mediaeval horn cores found in the motte and bailey at Castle Hill.

19

All Saints Parish Church in 1848 with the High Box pews and the Carrington
Gallery. From a painting by E.J. Niemann.

20

In Mind and Spirit

St Wulstan, Bishop of Worcester, consecrated the Church of All Saints some time between 1072 and 1092. Tradition suggests that he lodged here for six years. Smertlin, or Suarting, a wealthy Saxon 'of abundant fortune' who held the manor of nearby Bradenham at the time of Domesday, built the church.

The original building was cruciform in shape and only a fraction of the size of the present one, with the tower in the centre of the present nave instead of at the West End as now. High Wycombe was on the route from Windsor to Woodstock, and it was in Woodstock that King Henry II's mistress, Rosamond Clifford, died in 1176. She was buried at Godstow Abbey and among the many gifts that the sorrowing King showered on the Abbey was the advowson of the Church of High Wycombe, together with lands connected with it. This grant was confirmed by St Hugh, Bishop of Lincoln c1186. Godstow was an aristocratic establishment, and received the daughters of many leading citizens into its order. As late as 1538 a visitor noted that 'most of the young gentlewomen of the county were sent to be bred here'. Due to the royal patronage of the King, the tomb of the 'Fair Rosamond' was a treasured shrine, but in 1191 the Bishop of London, finding it adorned with silken hangings, rich lamps and candles, ordered the body to be buried outside the Abbey church in the Chapter House.

The lands belonging to Godstow Abbey in Wycombe lay in Frogmore, Crutchfield, Borsham and part of Townfield which was east and west of Crendon Lane. The Abbess was active in pursuing her rights, and in 1222 appealed to the King against Alan Basset. She was angered because he charged a payment of 4d a year on any new houses built on her land and he insisted that her men act as provers of bread and ale in the town. Finally when the Abbess's men collected dung and piled it up outside their houses, Alan Basset's men took it away and spread it on the fields as manure.

About this time the Burgesses sought justice against Alan Basset regarding their liberties which they asserted were embodied in a charter granted by Henry II. This was unfortunately deposited in the Church 'in the time of war and was burned with the Church'.

The houses that the Abbey owned faced the market and at that time the name Frogmore was used for the whole area from that point, along the side of the stream running from Frogmore to Hughenden. The Market itself was a triangle confined by Whitehart Street, Church Street and Queen's Square. In 1224 the Abbey owned two houses in Frogmore, six in a row near Temple Mill and two market booths.

By the end of the 13th century, the old Norman church walls were removed as the Chancel and Nave were lengthened, the North Chapel added to the Chancel and the aisles and South Porch built. In the 13th century a Chapel was added to the south side of the Chancel which became the Corporation Chapel. The South Porch was known as the 'Wedding Porch' and in his will, Christopher Wase, mayor in 1486, asked to be buried there. The South Chapel and the east window of the North Chapel are similar; when Sir John Stokton died in 1473, he left money for the extension of these chapels eastwards. The Bower Chapel was the North Chapel linked to Godstow Abbey, and the present South Chapel housed the Chapel of St Mary or Corporation Chapel. The Bower Chapel was founded c 1220 by Adam, son of Walder under the patronage of the Abbess of Godstow. It may have taken its name from John le Bowyer who left land to provide three wax candles, each 4lb in weight, to be burned on special saint   days.

Between 1468 and 1522 another elaborate rebuilding scheme was under way in which the burgesses undertook the raising of the arcades of the nave with its new roof and the widening of the North or Vicar's aisle to make room for the chapels and altars. There were six altars in 1519 and eight by 1526. The central tower posed a problem in the early 1500s as it obscured the view and damaged the acoustics of the altered church. On 26 January 1509 a contract was signed to take it down and rebuild that part of the Church. The West Tower was built between 1522 and 1535, and today's is said to have been designed by Rowland Messenger, Vicar of Wycombe in 1511, and a friend of Cardinal Wolsey. A will dated 1521 includes a bequest of 33s 4d towards the making of the steeple in the church, while another of 1535 bequeathed 'to the fynyshing of the stepall 3s 4d'.

The old central tower originally contained six bells which were supposed to be removed to the new tower on its completion. But in 1522 only '5 great bells' were listed. In 1711 there were again six bells, one undated and the others made between 1583 and 1683. These were taken to Spade Oak Wharf, Bourne End and travelled by river to Whitechapel where they were recast as eight bells. Later two more were added, the gifts of the sons of the Marquess of Lansdowne of Wycombe Abbey. The new clock was set in the tower in the 1870s with a new set of chimes playing seven tunes.

A further interior restoration took place in 1873-5 (architect G.E. Street), for £8,000, while the exterior restoration was completed by Oldrid Scott between 1887-9. The whole edifice was repaired with synthetic stone in the 1960-70s.

Of the chantries, most is known of the Corporation Chapel which was endowed by the Fraternity or Guild of St Mary. Four Wardens were responsible for the chapel, and in 1346 they included Thomas Gerveys who was Mayor of Wycombe twice, and who represented the Borough at Parliament seven times. The number of wardens had been reduced to two by 1517. The use of the Chantry is made clearer in the terms of a bequest of William Redhode, who was Mayor in 1475, in which he stated that the Priest of the Chantry Chapel had to 'pray for the good state, welfare and prosperity of all the tenants, men and women unto the said Chapel of Our Lady and for the good state, welfare and prosperity of William Redhode and Joan his wife and all their kindred being alive' and then to continue to pray for their souls after their death. William Redhode, for his part, gave a silver-gilt chalice bearing the words 'pray for the souls of Richard Redhode, Agnes his wife and William Redhode and Johanne his wife'. William Redhode also presented a wooden screen which still stands at the entrance to the Corporation Chapel with his inscription of 1468 carved on the chapel side. He additionally paid £14 for the repair of a house north of the churchyard for the Lady Priest and Bower Priest next to the house where the Priest of the Trinity Chapel lived. These were in the later Castle Street and stood next to the Priory (now Halfords). There is a path from these houses across the churchyard to a small door in the North side of the church. The penalty if the 'souls' were not paid for three days in a month was 4d.

When Joan Redhode died, she willed her best finger-ring to the image of Mary in the Chapel. Most of the burgesses and their wives seem to have belonged to this fraternity and its purpose was to ensure a continuous intercession for its members and so act as a kind of spiritual health service. The Borough diverted to its coffers a substantial proportion of the quit-rents which were due from most householders who were feudal tenants of the Corporation. It was also closely linked to the Mayor and the office of the Mayor, and in 1503 it was laid down that there should be no canvassing of members of the guild before the election of the new mayor, and that every burgess so offending was to be fined 20s, half of which went to the chantry.

At the time of the Reformation there was a mass removal of images and shrines. In 1547 John Bisse of Wycombe spoke out against this and was committed to Fleet Prison in London as he had 'spoken and doone inconveniently against the taking down of images abused in the Church of Wickham.' Some of the vestments, copes and plate were entrusted to the Mayor and eventually sold for £68, of which half 'was lost' and the remainder used for the town school. The Reformation sealed the fate of the Chantry Chapel of the Trinity. Three Londoners bought it, demolished it and cleared the site.

The church of St Lawrence at West Wycombe stands firmly on the site of the ancient hill fort and of the lost village of Haverington. John Wilkes commented 'Some churches have been built for devotion, others from parades of vanity. I believe this is the first church which has ever been built for a prospect...built on top of a hill for the convenience and devotion of the town at the bottom of it'. Tradition blames supernatural events for this, for the story goes how the stones and timbers gathered together to build the Church at the foot of the hill were twice mysteriously transported to the top at night. According to legend, the church was built where the material lay. The original building was mediaeval.

It appears that in 1537 the chancel was already in great need of repair and in 1650 records show that the windows were falling out, so when he restored the church, Sir Francis re-fashioned it more in keeping with his house. Thomas Phillibrown's diary for October 1752 notes that 'the tower of which Church Sir Francis has (at his own expense) for the sake of a prospect to his house and garden, raised to twice the height it was before and on top of the said tower is building a spire of timber, on the top of which is built of wood a very large hollow globe, the diameter of which is 8ft and the outside of it is to be covered with gilt'. He continued in July 1758 'it is very large and computed to hold 20 persons; there is a table in ye middle, seats around it and windows at the top. Sir Francis with 12 or 13 of his friends has been up in ye ball at one time and drank punch there'. Wilkes called the ball 'The best Globe tavern I was ever in'.

The interior of the church was also altered. Adjacent to the church on the east side is the large mausoleum open to the sky, built with money left to Lord le Despencer in 1762 by his friend George Dudington of Melcombe Regis. The Victorian church of St Paul was built in the garden of the Vicarage in 1846 of red brick with an apse and lancet windows.

Other parishes were created in the 19th century. The parish of Christchurch was formed in 1897, its church in Crendon Street and schoolroom in Queen Victoria Road; both have since disappeared. St John's in Desborough Road was consecrated in 1903 and designed by Caroe who did much work at Wycombe Abbey. St Anne's in Wycombe Marsh was built in 1858-61 in early Gothic style, while St James at Downley, designed by Cecil Brown and built in 1938-9 was never completed, but was replaced in the late 1970s by a dual purpose church. St Francis's at Terriers was designed by Sir Giles Gilbert Scott, and consecrated in 1930. Much more spectacular was the building of the church of St Mary and St George in Dashwood Avenue, which was designed by the Duke of Wellington in 1938, built of light brick and topped with an eye-catching green dome.

Prominent among early religious houses was the Hospital of St John the Baptist, the bare arches of which still stand in Easton Street. This was founded for a Master, Brethren and Sisters, and in 1239 Pope Gregory IX licensed the community to build its own chapel and appoint a chaplain. About 1230 the Burgesses of Wycombe undertook to see that 'The brethren and sisters shall every year for ever cause to be distributed bread made from two quarters of wheat to poor people coming to the Hospital for alms and charity'.

The funds for the hospital were modest, but in 1236 Richard of Rouen made a gift of his estate of 200 acres, which lay two miles down the valley. Even with this, the value of the whole endowment in 1516 was only £8. Henry III gave a grant which allowed the Hospital to hold an annual fair pitched in the east end of the town and held on the Feast and the Eve of the Translation of St Thomas a Becket (7 July). This fair was still going until 1527 when the Mayor and Burgesses invited 'all manner of pepuls for cum to the forsayde fayer free w'oute any manner of staullaydge payde that day to the bayllys'. By 1276 the Borough seems to have become the accepted patron of the Hospital and they presented the Wardens. Also when the son of a burgess assumed his hereditary right to the privileges of the Merchant Guild according to the ancient custom of the town, he paid dues of 10d to the borough official and ½d to the Hospital. This ½d was obtained on the 'lawday in the Rye holden the Thursday next after the Feast of St George' and if the Master of the Hospital was not present he forfeited the money. After some time the induction of new burgesses took place in the Guildhall and no part of the 10½d went to the Hospital.

The buildings still stand. Originally they fronted the south with the main hall, built c1175, standing north to south. On the Dissolution the Burgesses of Wycombe were not prepared to pass to the Crown the Lady Rents and other payments which had, by long tradition, been paid to the St Mary's Wardens. In March 1548, they resolved to protect their own and enacted that 'the Master Mayor and his brethren shall enter into the Hospital of St John's for the use of the town and for the relief of the poor according to the foundation thereof'.

However, matters got out of hand, because Christopher Chalfont, then Master of the Hospital, consigned the Hospital and its endowments to Sir Edmund Peckham and George Junklyn in return for an annual pension of £8. A month later Junklyn died, expressing the wish that the Hospital and its lands should be used to found and endow a grammar school. On 1 April 1549 the Hospital and its lands were conveyed to the Mayor and Burgesses of Wycombe for £30 on condition that the school be founded within two years. On 25 March 1551 they agreed on the payment of £8 a year to the incoming schoolmaster together with 'the pleasure and profit of a cow or tweyn on our common according to the custom of the town, and five loads of wood yearly'.

During the reign of Queen Mary the Burgesses managed to hold on to the St Mary rents, but on the accession of Queen Elizabeth, commissioners sought out 'concealed lands'. The Burgesses acted quickly, and on 18 July 1562 granted the Queen their rights in the Hospital. Three days later, on 21 July, the Queen in turn by letters patent gave them authority to found a grammar school and to establish a charity for the maintenance of four poor persons, and to finance this, she granted the town the Hospital of St John and the Lady rents.

The Hospital of St Margaret and St Giles lay south of the Rye, roughly where Wycombe Abbey is now. It is not shown in the borough records, nor received charitable bequests, for it was a leper hospital. The Lepers of Saint Giles of Wycombe were granted royal letters of protection in 1228, letters which urged all men to respond to their requests for charity. In 1229 they were also granted by Royal Charter the right to hold a fair for two days on the Eve and the Feast of St Margaret (20 July). Obviously the Hospital was in royal favour in the reign of Henry III for he also presented the lepers with ten oaks from his forest of Brill with which to repair the Hospital Chapel. The duration of this foundation is uncertain — in 1315 it was reported that the Brethren of the Hospital were accustomed to have a Warden 'of their own making' and as the establishment was in the hands of the King, the later masters were called 'King's Clerks'. By 1392 Richard May was granted the benefice of the Free Chapel of Saint Margaret, otherwise called the Hospital of Saint Giles, so its original function may have ceased, and it was then considered a chantry chapel. A later document records that Thomas Giles, a King's Clerk in the Royal Chapel of St Nicholas at Wallingford was appointed Warden in 1415. A century later, in 1516, Jacob Mallet, Canon of Windsor was Master of the Hospital of St Egidii (St Giles) in Wycombe Magna and resigned it to the College. However, his comments on the Dissolution 'that the King had brought his hogs to a fine market' caused him to be executed for treason in 1543.

The Borough was concerned with the plight of the poor following the Poor Law Act of 1601, and in 1605 they made bye-laws which forced newcomers to the Borough to provide guarantees, and they also made arrangements to apprentice orphan children. The indentures of 49 children from 1617 to 1696 indicate their thoroughness in this field. Due to the decline of the weaving industry and the competition in the lace industry more poor people came on to the rates. To distinguish them the Council ordered that they wear a badge on their upper garment in the form of a swan — later to be changed to the capital letter 'P' and the first letter of the name of their parish. The almshouses in Easton Street were falling into decay and in 1686, John Biggs, the Hospital Chamberlain rebuilt eight opposite the Grammar School. The original foundation stone has been preserved and states 'Ano Dom 1686 These Almshouses were built by order of ye Mayor and Court of Aldermen of the Corporation and finished by John Bigg. Senr Gent. Hospital Chamberlaine, for ye habitation of soe many poor people as ye major part of them in council shall think fit'. In 1727, as the Parish was without a workhouse, the Borough leased the Almshouse to the Churchwardens and overseers at a yearly rent of 5s and the next year converted them into a workhouse. The workhouse of the Wycombe Poor Law Union was built at Slough in the Saunderton Parish. A previous workhouse for the Union was in Bledlow which was the School of the Wycombe Poor Law Union by the 1860s. Inmates of the almhouses attached to the Grammar School received 8s per week but the almspeople in the other fourteen houses in the Borough only received 2s. The 18th century almshouses in Newland were rebuilt in Gordon Road in 1900. Only recently these were demolished and rebuilt on the opposite of the road.

There was always a conflict between the calls on the charity by the almshouses and by the School. The poet Edmund Waller (b1605) attended and, according to John Aubrey 'was bred under several ill, dull and ignorant schoolmasters, till he went to Mr Dobson at Wycombe, who was a good schoolmaster...I have heard Mr Thomas Bigge of Wycombe say that he little thought he would be so rare a poet'. Waller was to become Wycombe's representative in Parliament in 1626.

The school attracted some charities, and by the Will of Mary Bowden, proved 1790, monies were provided to pay £30 towards the salary of the Master of the Free Grammar School for the education of thirty or more boys aged from nine to fourteen and to teach them for three years. In July 1856 a new scheme for the management of the School was drawn up, and in 1865 James Poulter reported 'number increase and more space is needed'. This was remedied in 1882 when the new building in Easton Street was commenced. In the original plan the old mediaeval building was to be pulled down, with little protest from the town. In fact it was probably the outcry of the Society for the Protection of Ancient Buildings and of the Society of Antiquaries of London which influenced the architect Arthur Vernon to retain the arcading of the hall and the north wall of the chapel. The school was opened in September 1883. In only three decades this new building was again too small, and by 1908 a room was hired in the adjacent Congregational Church. In May 1914 Bishop Shaw laid the foundation stone of the new school at the top of Amersham Hill, where it still stands.

The Grammar School was not highly considered in the early 19th century: the 1833 Commission on Municipal Corporations heard that 'though more than a thousand children are educated in Wycombe schools supported by voluntary subscriptions, there was not a single scholar at the Free Grammar School'.

Earliest among other schools was the Royal Lancastrian which was established in 1813, and known after 1830 as the British School. This started in the old Manor House at Bassetsbury and had 180 boys. It moved to Church Street to house 100 boys and 180 girls. The National School, established by the Church of England in White Hart Street in 1855 taught 150 boys and 120 girls. A number of voluntary schools existed, at Bledlow (1868), Hazlemere (1847), West Wycombe Infants (1839) Wooburn (1852) and a Wesleyan day school was erected at Lane End in 1834.

Under the Elementary Education Act of 1870 the British School was transferred to the Borough School Board in February 1871. The Two Boards of the Parish and Borough of Chepping Wycombe combined to build a Central Board School in 1875 to accommodate 1,000 children. Built in Cemetery Road, it became known as the Priory Road Schools. With the Technical Instruction Act of 1889 a local committee was set up under which the School of Science and Art was built at Frogmore in 1893. The Wycombe High School for Girls' followed in September 1901.

In 1896 The Girls' Education Company, the culmination of a dream of Miss Francis Dove, was founded. This body negotiated to purchase Wycombe Abbey, the estate of Lord Carington, in May 1896. £20,000 was paid for the Abbey and thirty acres which surrounded it. The necessary alterations took place under the supervision of architect A.D. Caroe, and the school opened with 40 girls on 26 September 1896.

The Parish Church before the extensions to the tower by Henry Keene in 1775.

ABOVE: William Redhode's 1468 screen in front of the Corporation Chapel.
BELOW: The Parish church of All Saints, engraved by John Seago in 1786.

ABOVE: The Parish Church of All Saints, engraved by T. Lucas in 1845, and BELOW: the bells of All Saints in 1909 when they were removed for re-hanging.

ABOVE: The site of the priests houses in All Hallows Lane. BELOW: The
ruined arches of St John's Hospital, Easton Street.

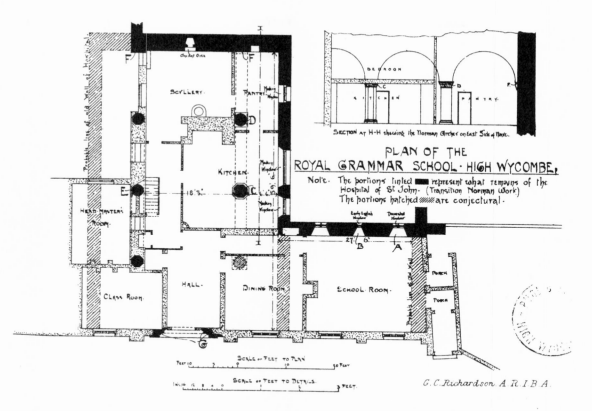

SECTION at H-H shewing the Norman Arches on East Side of Nave.

PLAN OF THE
ROYAL GRAMMAR SCHOOL · HIGH WYCOMBE.

Note. The portions tinted ▆▆▆ represent what remains of the
Hospital of St John. (Transition Norman Work)
The portions hatched ▨▨▨ are conjectural.

G. C. Richardson A.R.I.B.A.

ABOVE: A plan of the Grammar School, originally St John's Hospital, and
BELOW: the Grammar School c 1860.

31

ABOVE: The Royal Grammar School after the rebuilding in 1883. BELOW: The School in April 1915 at the top of Amersham Hill, designed by Arthur Vernon.

ABOVE: The Almshouses in Easton Street, and BELOW: a general view of
the Wycombe Union House, 1844.

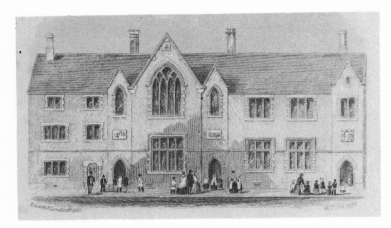

ABOVE LEFT: The National Schools in 1854. BELOW: Priory Road
Schools, opened in 1875, with RIGHT: Dame Frances Dove in 1896, the
headmistress of Wycombe Abbey School.

Mediaeval Borough

Domesday did not record the borough, but by the 1160s the men of Wycombe were 'farming' the manor and between 1181 and 1183 paid £4 a year to maintain the Borough's liberties. These were embodied in the Royal Charters which governed Borough action. The earliest record was a confirmation in 1237 of an earlier legal decision between the Burgesses and Alan Basset, which granted them the Borough of Wycombe together with rents, markets, fairs and fines. This charter was re-confirmed in 1825 by Edward I, in 1400 by Henry IV and in 1553 by Philip and Mary. The most important document was that of 1558 which was really a Charter of Incorporation, confirming previous rights, including the freedom from toll throughout England, the power to purchase lands, hold courts and to elect officers. Other charters were granted by succeeding monarchs which added or changed powers and privileges. Seven of these historic charters have survived.

The earliest Officers of the Borough were the three bailiffs who were elected from the Burgesses. In the mid 13th century the office of Mayor was established, with Roger Hutred or Outred in office from about 1285 to 1303, and from that date the office has been continuous. The Mayor was elected annually on the Thursday before Michaelmas and with the powers of the Charter of 1558 became Justice of the Peace, Coroner and Clerk of the Market, while the Council itself held the Assize of bread, wine and ales, measures and weights, treasure trove...in fact everything connected with the daily commercial life of the town. When he was elected, the Mayor had several expenses to pay.

Connected with the election are the customs of 'tolling out' and the more well known 'weighing in'. The former, which ceased with the Municipal Corporation Act, arose from the behaviour of Henry Shepard in 1678 for 'insolently misbehaving himselfe, by beinge drunke and offring affronts to sev'all gentlemen...in token whereof it is ordered that the Great Bell shall be rung out accordinge to custome, in testimony of his misdemeanours'. Thus the outgoing Mayor was 'tolled out' and the Corporation would proceed to St Mary's Chapel and on their return across the streets they would tread on the flowers which had been strewn, preceded by the drummer. They then went to the Guildhall to choose the new Mayor, after which the Corporation went in procession round the Market Hall, the new Mayor was drummed into office and the church bells pealed to let the townsfolk know a new Mayor had been elected. After luncheon came the weighing in ceremony, which now takes place in the yard in front of The Falcon.

Here, starting with the Mayor, all the Council are weighed and as their weights are called out by the Beadle, the words 'and some more' added if the Mayor has gained weight, and 'and no more' if he is of the same weight or less. The spectators wait for the call, and if the words 'and some more' are heard the person being weighed is jeered as he goes back to his place, having grown fat at the expense of the ratepayers. This ceremony is believed to go back to mediaeval times, but fell into disuse after the Reform Act and was revived in 1892. The heaviest weight recorded was in 1960 when Counciller R.A. Wood weighed in at 20 stone 5lb.

The Mayor and Alderman did not always receive the respect to which they were accustomed. In 1662 William Child, an attorney from Chesham, derided the Borough Charters and their powers in the Guildhall Court, saying 'you make your charter a nose of wax' and continued against the Mayor and the aldermen in the Maidenhead Inn in Crown Lane, saying to a Justice of Peace (the Mayor) 'a turd for you' and as for the rest of the Court of Aldermen 'a turd for them all'. For these insults an order prohibiting him from practising in Wycombe Courts was agreed on 28 August 1662.

The status of Burgess was hereditary and the ownership or occupation of a house, or of a door opening on to High Street was the original requirement. In 1226 there were twenty-six burgesses who witnessed the legal contract between the Borough and Alan Basset. The Mayor might elect notable persons as burgesses, and on one occasion in 1672 he elected eighty-five new burgesses in order that he might influence the election of the next Mayor. Within twenty days of election a Burgess had to deliver a leather bucket for the use of the Corporation, to be kept in the Town Hall. When the Burgess was chosen for office, the first year he was a Gelden or Gildan. This duty was uncertain, but appears to ensure that the tenants of the Borough only pastured the correct number of cattle on the Rye. The second year the Burgess would be a Churchwarden, the third a Constable and the fourth a Bayliffe. The Bailiffs by an order of 1595 were required to wear a gown at the Court Leet under penalty of £20.

The Aldermen were elected from among the Burgesses, but are not mentioned in the records until the 16th century, and by the Charter of 1609 were limited to twelve. The Town Clerk's position also dated from the 17th century while that of High Steward was created by the 1558 Charter and abolished in 1609 when the Office of Recorder was introduced. The Sergeant-at-Mace dates back to the 14th century, at which time he received ½d on the election of a Burgess or Guildsman.

Other officers in the early days included the Hospital Chamberlain who was responsible for the Hospital of St John the Baptist, the Beadle and Town crier, The Hayward, the Head Constable, the Surveyor, Inspector of Nuisances, Collector of the Market Tolls, besides the more important position of Treasurer. The Head Constable in later years was also the Inspector of weights and measures.

The office of High Steward was instituted in the Charter of Philip and Mary and the occupants of that honour included Major General Thomas Scott in 1651, the regicide who signed King Charles' death warrant and in 1686 George Lord Jefferies, Lord High Chancellor of England known as 'the very worst judge that ever disgraced

Westminster Hall'. A rather more lowly office was that of the Tithingmen. These were petty constables who acted in the two Tithings, areas formed by the manors of Temple Wycombe and Bassetsbury which fell outside the boundaries of the Borough and which together formed the 'forrens'. Their duties were not so precisely laid down as those of the Borough constables, but at the time of election of the mayor, the four Tythingmen came in for their reward of 2s 6d each.

The documents of the Borough are in the form of minutes of Council, Treasurer accounts and reports and accounts of the different officers or committees in some cases going back to mediaeval times. The First Ledger Book contains the reports of the Council and was given to the Corporation by William Redhode, Mayor in 1475. This handsome volume of 240 parchment leaves was the first of several Leger books which recorded the happenings in the Council Meetings of the Wycombe Borough. Borough documents were sealed with the Town Seal, and when the Borough was involved in a suit with Ralf de la Lude in 1407, the award was sealed with the Common Seal of the Town. This was later clarified, for in the early 18th century it was ordered that 'the towne seale shall always remayn in the tresurye, upon payne and penaltie of Clb [£100] to be levied upon the goods and catalls at the Maier for the tyme beinge for not fullinge of this order'. There were three seals; the oldest one of wood was circular and 1⅜" in diameter, bearing the device of a swan ducally gorged and the motto 'BURGVS DE CHEPINGE WYCOMBE IN COM BVCK'. The second seal was an oval one of silver, 1¼" long, and similar to the wooden one. The third seal is the embossing stamp and a facsimile of the silver oval seal. This was probably destroyed on the blacksmith's anvil in 1946, when the High Wycombe Corporation came into existence.

The Borough was proud of its regalia, some of which dates back to Stuart Times. The earliest Mace was probably Elizabethan. A later mace was purchased in 1633 for £20, out of money bequeathed to the Borough. As this money was intended for the poor, there were hard feelings about the transaction, and a sum known as 'Mace Money' was annually paid back. This continued until 1962, when it amounted to £1 3s 4d annually. The Borough received a new mace in 1694, made of silver-gilt and 4ft 7in long, known nowadays as the Great Mace. This was the donation of Thomas Lewes or Lewis and Charles Godfrey, who were Members of Parliament at the time. The new mace bore their coats of arms, that of the Borough and the Royal Coat of Arms of William and Mary. Until the recent Local Government Re-organisation of 1974 it represented the Monarch in the Borough processions. The earlier mace was sold about 1696 to cover the costs of a legal suit. A further 'small mace' dates from 1687 when it was purchased at a cost of £1 17s 6d.

Also dating from 1694 is the silver walking stick used by the Mayor in processions. It is 3ft 2¾in long with the arms of the Borough on the flat top, and was also given by Thomas Lewes and Charles Godfrey, probably to replace the iron stick given by William Fleetwood in 1576. He was Recorder of the City of London.

The Town Crier's badge is an oval one of silver 4½ inches by 3½ inches marked for 1685-6 and its design consists of the chained swan of Wycombe within a border of laurel leaves. This badge, the Swan of Bucks, originated in the 12th century and was used by the de Bohun Family, who held lands in Buckinghamshire which included Wycombe. The Swan was used on the Wycombe Town arms, and in 1566 it was recorded during a Visitation of the Clarenceux Herald, when it was described as a Swan with closed wings on a black ground. An addition to the normal regalia is the 18th century Town Drum, used in mayor-making ceremonies, and purchased by the Town Chamberlain in the 18th century. Following changes in the Borough in the 1870s, several items have been added, including the Mayor's chain.

Although the constitution of the Corporation had been formalised by the 13th century and consisted of the Mayor and Bailiffs, there were also elder or leading Burgesses who were simply termed the Brethren of the Mayor. It was established in 1498 that the Mayor should be elected from among this body. The group together with the Mayor was known as The Counsel House and all were elected by the community, and not nominated by the Mayor as in later years. The Borough Election days and Lawdays were held on the Rye. On these Lawdays leases were renewed, fresh grants made and new byelaws passed. That the Lawday took place in the open indicates the democratic nature of the mediaeval borough in which the Commonalty, or ordinary man in the street had his part to play. The Council also met in the Guild-Hall to deal with more everyday affairs, and this building or its predecessors date back at least to the 13th century. In 1380 the 'solarium' or gallery at the end of the Guildhall was leased to John Deye at an annual rent of 3s 4d. It is possible that it was on the site of an old building demolished in 1930, which stood behind the buildings opposite the West Door of the Church. There was also a building referred to in leases of 1477 as the Elde Yeld Hall (the Old Guild Hall). In 1711 the Corporation leased to Isaac Bailey the Old Guildhall 'with the shops, upper rooms and pent houses and the ground under the same penthouses and the lofts and rooms over the common prison or Counter or Clapper Cott adjoining...except for the prison itself and Clapper Cott and free passage into and from the said shops for the lifting and drawing up and shutting down of the gate in the Dungeon under the said shops'. The building demolished in 1930, known as the Old Guildhall, was formerly on the site of Lyons Shop in Church Street, opposite the entrance to the new Wycombe Fayre and formed part of the open space which was the original Market space.

Under the will of Sir John Stokton, made in 1470-73, monies were left for a market house to be built on the south side of High Street, probably on the present site. It was to be a wooden structure, built on oaken posts, and it could have been completed c1480. L.J. Ashford feels it possible that this Market House was rebuilt in 1604, repaired in 1711 and then replaced by the present brick and stone building in 1757.

The Guildhall was used for the meetings of the Council, but the meetings were frequently adjourned in order that its members might carry on business in the greater comfort of the Swan or the Catherine Wheel. It was used for business other than Council matters, such as drawing up trade ordinances, inquests and as a Court of Law. There is a 16th century order which states 'it is ordeyned ...the geldhall dor shall be stondying opyn freely where as ony burgess be committed to ward …and inspeciall that other burgess may have licens to exorte and advise hym to the beste'. (When a burgess is on trial, the other burgesses have the right to come to the proceedings and advise the defendant of his legal position.)

When Lord Shelburne was elected as Parliamentary Member for the Borough the Corporation was concerned about the condition of the Guildhall. It had made alterations in 1733 and constructed a 'handsome and convenient' room to serve as a Council Chamber. When Lord Shelburne indicated his willingness to build a new one, his offer was accepted. The architect was Henry Keen, and by October 1757 the Earl's Steward was able to report that 'the roof of the Market House is up, and part of the cornish [cornice], which looks very pretty, and adds beauty to the whole structure'. Not everyone was so satisfied, for Joe Shrimpton, who was Mayor in 1740, 1753, 1763 and 1755 grew 'mad to have the roof covered with glazed tiles' such as those obtainable from Gerrards Cross.

The building also had its problems; the riots of 1830 had caused much damage and in 1845 money was spent to provide new seating, and the locks and fastenings of the doors needed renewing, as well as the rope for the market bell. In 1859 the Guildhall was thoroughly renovated with the help of a gift of £150 from Sir G.H. Dashwood, Bart. who was at the time Member of Parliament for High Wycombe. More restoration took place in the early 1970s in which metal support pillars were inserted to help the stone pillars of 1757 in their task of supporting the main building. The latest Town Hall was built in the newly opened Queen Victoria Road and erected to designs of J.J. Bateman and C.E. & A. Hale in 1904. It was equipped with a stage and an organ installed in 1905. Modernisation took place in 1972-3. This building took over the social functions of the previous Town Hall which reverted once again to the title of Guildhall, and a new Municipal Building, opened in 1932 in Queen Victoria Road, provided accommodation for the Council Staff and a Council Chamber.

A document issued by the Wycombe Burgesses c 1230.

ABOVE LEFT: Extract from the mediaeval illuminated manuscript of a legal treatise which forms part of the First Ledger book in the Borough Archives. CENTRE: A contemporary picture of Queen Elizabeth I in the initial letter of the 1598 Charter, RIGHT: the Charter of James II, 1685. BELOW LEFT: William Redhode's inscription in the First Ledger Book, presented to the Borough in 1475. CENTRE: The Great Mace, showing the monogram of William and Mary. RIGHT: The Mayor in procession in 1908.

ABOVE LEFT: Queen Elizabeth II viewing the Town Charters in 1962.
RIGHT: A wooden corbal from the old Guildhall, showing the Chepping
Wycombe Borough Arms, and BELOW: a drawing of the Guildhall prior to
rebuilding in the 18th century.

42

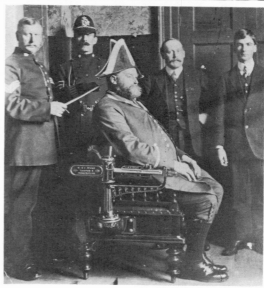

ABOVE: The Guildhall by E.J. Niemann, c 1830, showing the Mayor and
Council in procession. BELOW LEFT: The arms of Chepping Wycombe
Borough, as recorded in 1634 and confirmed by Chester Herald in 1920.
RIGHT: The weighing-in of the mace bearer, c 1910.

Weighing-in of the Mayor, Geoffrey H. Baker in 1947, using the new scales.

Industry Enriches

The Borough's motto 'Industry Enriches' confirms nine hundred years of industrial and commercial progress, and it also emphasises the fact that the furniture industry, which most consider the basis of the town's prosperity, is only the latest of a series of industries which have been exploited over the centuries. For the first we must go back to the Domesday report of 1086, to Wycombe's mills on the river. It was also the centre of the wool trade from the time of the Conquest to the 1700s and this was due largely to the pasture lands on the slopes along the valley, to the presence of fuller's earth in the ground and once again the mills. The Abbess of Godstow claimed tithes on nine mills in the 13th century with some of the tithes coming in the form of linen and hemp. Traders settled in Wycombe, and by 1221 the cloth industry was well established. There are references to workmen, such as William FitzJohn, weaver, and Andrew the Linen Draper, in the Charter of 1270. Nicholas the Dyer got married about 1241 and Christina of Wycombe met her death by falling into a boiling dying vat in 1227. The fulling mills in 1235 were held by Marten Fuller, and when a new fulling mill was planned at Loudwater, it was considered a threat to the town, the lease stipulating that no cloth made in or delivered to Wycombe for treatment by fullers could be handled by this mill.

The rough wool from which the local cloth was made did not match up to that produced in adjacent counties, but this was not necessarily a drawback. In 1306 the Sheriff of Beds and Bucks was ordered to buy in Wycombe and elsewhere sixty pieces of rough webbed cloth for covering tents in Edward's last Scottish campaigns. The Guild of Wycombe was almost inseparable from the Council, and it charged 12d a year for the use of each loom where the trade of weaving was exercised in the Borough. For a further 2d, the weaver could be eligible for all the rights of a guild merchant. In order to encourage the foreign weavers (from outside the Borough) at one time, this fine of 12d was remitted in 1316 with only stallage charged. To ensure the continuance of the craft, apprentices were encouraged. In 1400, John Justicere, a weaver by trade, took as apprentice John Griffyn from Cardigan. The indenture ensured that Griffyn bound himself to serve his master and his master's interest for three years, and in return he was to be taught the 'mystery' of weaving. It was decided in 1510 that no weavers or fullers could practice in the borough unless they had been apprenticed.

Edward III, in his effort to build up the wool industry, encouraged foreign craftsmen to help raise the standard of English weaving. He also forbad the export of wool in order to make sure that there were sufficient supplies for the home market. But some highly placed merchants were able to get round this law. In 1342 William de Bohun, Lord of the manor of Wycombe, was granted a licence to export 200 sacks of wool to Brittany, each sack of 26 stone charged at 2s per stone. The foreign weavers included John Weitzer, a Flemish immigrant from Brabout who bound himself to be apprenticed in 1424 to William Brabayn of Wycombe, and in 1436 two other Flemish weavers living in Wycombe, John de Clyf of Brabant and John Caller, born in Liege, were granted licences to 'dwell peacably and enjoy their goods in the Borough'.

There was a rapid growth in the local wool industry, and the Guild and Borough found things getting out of hand, for a new category of industrialist who employed craftsmen rather than working himself began to appear. This worried the Council who in 1511 ordered that 'no person occupying the crafts of occupations of weaving, fulling or dyeing shall...meddle more than in and of one of the same occupations'. They were ordered to put out their work, the clothiers to the weavers, as the clothier supplied the yarn and marketed the cloth; the weaver must then pass the woven cloth to the fuller who added the finish to the material, and he in turn must pass the cloth to the dyer for completion. The 1558 Charter encouraged local participation in the cloth trade as it stipulated that no one who did not belong to the Guild 'shall sell or buy flax, wool or thread, skin or hide within the borough' and in 1606, action against outsiders was emphasised when a special tax of 6d was levied on every foreign loom, and to tie up the industry completely, George Bradshaw paid 20s yearly to exclude foreign dyers from practising in the Borough. But the end of the cloth industry was in sight, and in 1623 the Justices and Mayor of Wycombe reported that the 'trades of clotheings and Bone Lace makeinge are much decayed and doe daylie fayle, the poore are greatlie hindered and impoverished'.

The fullers may have suffered earlier than this date from the loss of their trade; two fulling mills were on the river at Bassetsbury in 1411 and in 1620 Gosham's Mill, the La Lude Mill, later known as Raunce's Mill and Loudwater Mill were still used for this purpose. The cloth industry had ceased to be of importance in this area by the mid 17th century. Although wool had ceased to be part of the clothing trade, wool fairs were still carried on in the Borough up to the 19th century, with the Wool Fair re-established in 1838 on the last Wednesday in June. This Fair was held under the Guildhall and the Market House. It continued until 1844, and in 1861 the Directory reports that the 'annual Wool Fair has fallen into disuse'.

The grain trade and the corn market grew out of the normal supply of wheat for the locality, but by the 13th century, it was obvious that the large number of mills and the wheat harvest in the area raised this above that level. According to the records of the Bishop of Winchester, Wycombe was one of the largest producers of wheat among the 32 manors belonging to the Winchester Estates in 1208. It was also at times the largest supplier of oats, showing a better return for the seed sown than any other villages on the estate.

Baking in itself was a minor local industry, as the Borough frequently supplied large quantities for the Royal Household. In 1241 Henry III sent orders for 100s of bread at four loaves to the penny to be supplied to the Royal Palace of Westminster at Christmas, and again in 1245 £10 of bread (over 500 loaves) was supplied for the Feast of St Edward. In 1248 the town was fined 2 marks, and an extra charge of 20s on the bakers themselves for either not supplying the bread, or because it was not to the satisfaction of the Court.

Such large orders had to be transported by road, and the condition of these roads was a factor essential to the corn trade. Realising this, Sir John Stokton left £40 in his will for the repair of the road through Wycombe from Holtspur to West Wycombe, but even more important to the grain trade was his bequest stipulating that a covered market house be built for the sale of corn on the south side of the High Street. The ground floor was to be open to the front facing the High Street, while the upper floor, which was to be supported on timber posts, was to contain granaries. At the back was to be a staircase leading to the granaries, and under this staircase the standard grain measures of the bushel, half bushel, peck and half peck were to be stored. This, according to L.J. Ashford, was the real establishment of the Wycombe corn market. In 1489 at a Lawday on the Rye, it was enacted that all comers should be able to buy grain in Wycombe without paying toll.

The nearness of Wycombe to London meant that it was within the range of corn-dealers, called badgers, who would travel down and compete with the local traders, so pushing prices above those of other similar markets further afield. This had the effect of making the market popular with farmers, and they would come in from adjacent counties. In 1630, when there was a nationwide shortage of food, an attempt was made by the Privy Council to hold the price of grain below the normal market level. When this was tried at Wycombe, the London corn-dealers refused to buy as they knew they would be forced to re-sell at a loss, and the farmers who had come to sell found the fixed prices also to their disadvantage. Later in 1631 a survey of the district found there was insufficient grain to meet local demand, yet due to the high prices still found at Wycombe, the market had plenty. By this time the toll had been set on the sale of corn and during the 17th and 18th centuries, the revenue from this and other tolls played an important part in the Borough's finances. In the mid 17th century tolls produced about £50 per annum, but by 1699 £70 was raised and in 1751 the tolls were let for £130, while in 1772 they raised £253 and in 1781 £277.

The toll was taken in grain and was originally one quart to a bushel, reduced to a pint to a bushel in the Napoleonic Wars due to increased prices and when they settled back the product of the toll was so little that after 1832 it was down to £20 a year. This 'toll-corn' as it was called, was sold on the open market, and the price varied from 38s a quarter in 1822 to 81s a quarter in the next year. The amount of grain sold in the market has been assessed for 1821 when 42½ quarters of toll-corn were sold, which at a pint per sack represents a sale of 21,760 sacks sold at the Wycombe Market in one year.

The Buckinghamshire lace industry is reputed to have had its origins with Katharine of Aragon. Thread-lace had been made in England as early as 1463 and bone-lace or pillow-lace was mentioned in 1577. In 1611 a complaint was laid against men 'who continuallie travelled to sell bone-lace on the Sabbath Day' and between 1618 and 1686 the Overseers to the Poor and Churchwardens in the Borough of Wycombe placed nine orphan children as apprentices in bone-lace making. In 1623 the lace industry was depressed, but by 1680 the lacebuyers had organisd themselves into a working industry. One of the merchants was Ferdinando Shrimpton of Penn who petitioned against the costly hawker's license required to carry on his lace business. As the cost of such a licence would fall heavily on others in the Borough, a petition was drawn up which stated that Ferdinando Shrimpton and others 'follow bone-lace making in the wholesale way by keeping several hundred workmen constantly employed...These wholesale men trade weekly to London where they sell their lace and then buy thread and silk which they bring home to their workmen...who every week deliver to their respective masters who pay the workmen what they have earned.'

A further petition signed by other lacemen in the County was sent to the House of Commons in which they stressed that it was through their promotion of the manufacture of bone-lace that 'thousands of poor persons and those of tender years are able to get their livings'. An Act then exempted lacemen from holding such licences. Lace schools were opened. Buckinghamshire lace was originally in old Flemish style, but in 1778 'point-ground' was introduced from which the traditional Bucks pillow lace developed and it was used chiefly for baby lace and edgings. The wages paid in 1794 were about 1s - 1s 6d per day, but by 1813 these had dropped to 9d - 1s 4d per day. The Patron Saint of lacemakers was St Katherine, and apparently the Saint's Day (25 November) was observed as a holiday in Wycombe with Cattern cakes being made for the occasion. The Katherine Wheel Inn, formerly in High Street, took its name from the industry. The stained glass windows in the Town Hall commemorate Daniel Hearn as the developer of the lace industry, though he appeared towards the end of its course. He had lived in Easton Street where the Union Chapel now stands, and developed the village industry of lacemaking by collecting the lace, and opening a London warehouse for its disposal. He purchased the site of the old Katherine Wheel Inn which had been destroyed by fire about 1780 and erected, c1837, the premises in High Street which he named Buckingham House, but which the lacemakers christened 'Bobbin Castle', now the location of W.H. Smith & Son. The introduction of John Heathcoat's 'Bobbin' machine of 1809 made traditional lacemaking uneconomic and the lace industry was doomed. With the introduction of the Education Act in 1870 came the end of the lace schools as the Board School took their place.

The straw plait industry came into being in this county in the 1720s and it was locally practised by the 1770s. The census of 1801 indicates that a large part of the population was engaged in lace making and straw plaiting and by 1813 their popularity caused a shortage of female labour for agricultural work. The import of the finer foreign plaits was forbidden during the Napoleonic Wars, so encouraging local industry, and in 1813 a woman was able to earn 30s a week.

In High Wycombe lacemaking was almost entirely superseded by straw plaiting and in 1861 there was a large number of plait makers in the town. In 1833 there were several makers of straw hats in Wycombe, who would have been dependent on the straw plait made by these workers. Mary Ann Palmer and Mary Dulley were in the High Street, Sophia Maynard in the Market Place, James Bird in Paul's Row, Sarah Wright in Oxford Road and Elizabeth and Sarah Gilbert in Temple Place. By 1877 the demand had created plait schools at a charge of one penny a week for the learner. Within the trade there were bleachers, cutters, dyers, flatters, stringers, drawers and packers. The local straw plait industry operated between 1750 and 1900.

Papermaking had spread to Buckinghamshire in the late 16th century. Glory and Lower Mills were both let at £50 per annum in 1627 and a new mill at Loudwater was let in 1638 for the same amount. The failure of the cloth-making trade in High Wycombe had released mills with fulling machines, which could be used for making pulp out of rags, while the water of the Wye river was free from iron salts or other impurities which might discolour the paper. Easy access to the Thames meant that barges could bring the waste rags down from London for conversion into paper.

Local opinion was against the new industry and in 1632 a letter was sent to the Privy Council complaining against the constant noise of the hammers in the mills which pounded the rags into pulp and which continued working even on Sundays. They also complained against the stench of the rags, but, above all, about the danger of plague. In 1631 between April to September, fifty six persons died in High Wycombe from the plague, almost half of all deaths. In 1636 there had been another serious outbreak and paper mills within ten miles of Windsor were forbidden to obtain rags from London. In the 1690s it was claimed that eight mills in the Parish of High Wycombe employed fifty families making white paper. Although the Wycombe paper was not generally watermarked and so recognisable, it was stated in 1775 by Daniel Defoe to be 'very good of its kind and cheap, such as generally is made use of in printing or newspapers, journals, etc., and smaller pamphlets; but not much fine or large for bound books or writing'. One authority considered that the Wye Valley mills were one of the principal sources of newsprint for the London market. While the mills from Wycombe to Loudwater were involved in making white paper, those lower down the Wye River were making boards.

A report of 1832 reports 'there are also several paper mills near the town and in different parts of the Parish which give employment to about 300 persons. We understand that this business has much declined of late in consequence of its being carried on principally by hand. The machinery which is now generally used in paper mills has been adopted in only two of the mills of the neighbourhood'.

The change came gradually, and another report notes 'at one time there were in and around Wycombe no less that 28 vats at work all of which have disappeared'. Not only were there changes in the methods, but materials were altered.

These changes brought anger as well as apprehension on the part of the workmen, as the machines replaced the hand processes. In the autumn of 1830 farm machine riots caused the local paper workers to consider similar action. A group met in the Rye in November 1830, moved to the Guildhall and broke up a meeting of prominent townspeople before marching to Ash Mill with the intention of smashing the machinery. As chance would have it, a troop of Bucks Yeomanry was in the vicinity, and this enraged the papermakers, the disturbances continuing until the Riot Act was read and the men melted away. Meetings were held over the weekend and once more they met and marched on Ash Mill where they forced their way into the mill, and then went on to Marsh Green Mill, where the machinery was thoroughly wrecked. In the middle of this the Riot Act was once again read, and the men went on to other mills causing damage until the special constables, having bided their time until the men were either drunk or disillusioned, arrested the ringleaders and others involved, with forty nine ending up in Aylesbury Prison awaiting trial.

A special Commission began on 10 January 1831, and John Sawney and Thomas Blizzard were condemned to death and twenty two had the 'Judgement of Death' announced, which really meant transportation. Eventually the death sentences were commuted to transportation also, and they went to Botany Bay. In the campaign to stop the hangings, 'The sorrowful lamentation of Thomas Blizzard and John Sawney' was published which urged 'We hope you will a warning take all you who come to see these most wretched men hanging on the tree'.

Despite these set-backs, the industry prospered and for the papermakers who remained in employment, the average wages increased by at least 25%, although the smaller manufacturers were gradually eliminated and the large mills persisted with only ten in operation in the 1930s. In 1936 Marsh Mill became known as Wycombe Marsh Paper Mills, and was modernised. During the Second World War the mill concentrated on the production of ammunition papers, and since then an expansion with coated papers took place which culminated in a purpose built coating plant in 1972.

The control over craftsmen and shop-keepers in mediaeval Wycombe was rigidly applied in favour of Guildsmen or Burgesses of the Borough. The Wycombe traders who worked from the High Street or Markets were concerned that their privileges should not be breached and so they did their best to prevent foreign traders from taking up residence in the Town and selling their products in the Market. In 1564 the shoemakers paid 20s yearly to the Bailiff to stop others selling shoes in the town, in 1577-8 all foreign maltsters paid ½d on every quarter of malt they made, in 1610 tailors paid 10s to keep out other tailors, and about the same time the hatmakers and hat sellers paid 6s 8d yearly for the same privilege.

The Market itself was held from early times on a Friday and the stalls were in the Hogmarket where there was probably some kind of covered building before the Shambles was built in 1622, which preceded the present Market House. The legal contract between Alan Basset and the Borough in 1237 granted to the Burgesses the right to hold a market and fairs, and the Borough ran the market from then on. In 1766 the Council ruled that 'the Cryer's Bell shall be rung at ten o'clock in the forenoon upon every Market day for this Borough for the selling of fish, butter, cheese, sheep, lambs, calves, swine, pigs, geese, capons, ducks, turkeys, hens, chicken, pigeons and rabbits and that if any Higler or forrigner or other person or persons buing the same to sell again...before the said bell shall ring...shall forfeit the value of the goods and things so bought'.

Besides the weekly markets there were annual fairs, and the first mention is in 1226 when the annual cattle fair was said to have been held on the land of Alan Basset. The Borough had two fairs granted by the Charter of 1558, one on St Thomas's Day, 7 July and the other on 14 September, the Feast Day of the Exaltation of the Holy Cross. They took place from noon on the Eve of the Feast until noon on the day of the Feast itself. Other fairs were held by the Hospital of St John the Baptist on his Feast Day (24 June) and by the Hospital of St Margaret (20 July). In 1663 four fairs were held in the borough, on 24 June, 14 September, 28 October and the Saturday before Lent. Horse and cattle fairs were held in the Borough in April and October, and following a deputation to the Council in 1838, these were revived.

The Charter Fair, held on the Monday and Tuesday before Michaelmas was locally known as the Wycombe Hiring Fair, for labourers came to the town to be hired for the coming season. The abolition of the Hiring Fair was called for in the 1870s, because of the charge that it was a 'fruitful source of immorality and crime, as well as being a serious injury to the commercial prosperity of the town and neighbourhood', Others feared that if abolished, there would be great inconvenience to the labourers, for in 1872, men came to Wycombe to be hired. These hiring fairs carried on annually until about 1908.

In January 1824 'a man led a women, who, he said was his wife, with a rope and halter round her neck, into Chepping Wycombe cattle market and offered her for sale. She was pushed into the sale ring with the cattle and was quickly purchased by a man, a Blacksmith, who offered 10s for her as she stood. The Woman was by no means unpleasing and appeared to be a little over 25 years of age. Her only clothing was a sack tied round her neck and above her knees. The Collector of Tolls demanded, and received, from the purchaser the customary 1d paid on sold live stock'.

Bushel measure, 1672, purchased because the Mayor and Council were summoned at Assizes for not having a bushel.

51

16th *SEPTEMBER*, 1800.

WE whofe Names are hereunto fet,

Taking into our moſt ſerious Confideration,

THE ALARMING,

Unprecedented, and unaccountable

HIGH PRICE of BREAD CORN,

Do earneſtly Recommend to all

FARMERS, and other Perſons having Corn,

That they will uſe all Diligence to bring a Large Supply to the Markets for the Uſe of the BAKERS, and SUFFERING POOR,

And unqueſtionably this muſt be their *true Intereſt*,

As the preſent EXTRAVAGANT PRICES cannot continue Long.

And We do alſo Recommend to all

Mealmen, and Other Perſons having Mills, or

DEALING IN CORN,

That they will have the Goodneſs not to Purchaſe any BREAD CORN, but barely to Supply their current Buſineſs from Week to Week, and ſuch as have a Stock, to refrain from purchaſing any until Wheat ſhall be fallen greatly under the preſent Prices, and which we truſt the Stock of the Country muſt inevitably very ſhortly effect, of courſe it muſt be their intereſt alſo to follow the Recommendation we have taken the Liberty to give them, beyond the humanity of the Meaſure itſelf.

J. Daſhwood King,	Samuel Welles,	James Batting,
William Clayton,	Thomas Clarke,	Adey Bellamy,
J. Hicks,	Samuel Manning,	Henry Allnutt,
James Price,	Thomas Roſe,	Samuel Edmonds,
Iſaac King,	A. E. Biddle,	William Baly.

High-Wycombe : Printed by S. *CAVE*, at the *Printing-Office*, near the Church.

A poster in 1800 about the alarmingly high price of bread corn.

52

ABOVE: The Market under the Market House, drawn by the Officers of the
Royal Military College, c 1800. BELOW: The Friday cattle market behind
the Guildhall in Paul's Row, c 1900.

ABOVE: The sheep outside the shops in Church Street, c 1900. BELOW LEFT: The Hiring Fair outside the Guildhall, 1905, and RIGHT: the Water Mill on the Wye.

ABOVE: Bridge Mill, St Mary Street, BELOW LEFT: Bonnet mould at the
Museum, and RIGHT: preparing the plaiting straws.

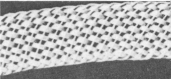

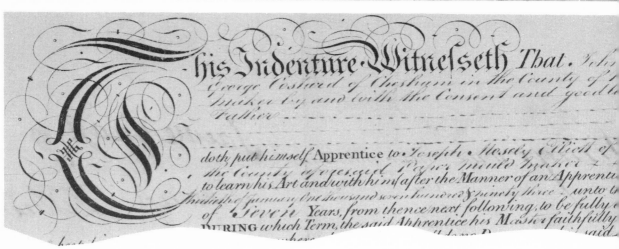

56

ABOVE: Three examples of plaits: the wholestraw plait, brilliant split plait and English wave, black and white plait. CENTRE LEFT: Mrs Dobbin's lace school at Stokenchurch c 1860 and RIGHT: Mrs Amos Ray, lacemaker of Penn, c 1900, with CENTRE: tokens in use in High Wycombe. BELOW: Part of the apprenticeship indenture for John Costard, to be taught the art of a paper-mould maker under Joseph Mosely Elliott of Wycombe Marsh, 10 January 1795.

CALENDAR OF THE PRISONERS,

In His Majesty's Gaol at Aylesbury,

FOR FELONIES & MISDEMEANOURS,

Who have taken their Trials at the Session of Oyer and Terminer and Special Gaol Delivery, holden at AYLESBURY, on MONDAY the TENTH Day of JANUARY, 1831, before THE HONOURABLE SIR JAMES ALLAN PARK, KNIGHT, one of the Judges of His Majesty's Court of Common Pleas; THE HONOURABLE SIR WILLIAM BOLLAND, KNIGHT, one of the Barons of His Majesty's Court of Exchequer; and THE HONOURABLE SIR JOHN PATTESON, KNIGHT, one of the Judges of His Majesty's Court of King's Bench.

Richard William Howard Howard Vyse, Esquire, Sheriff.

No.

1. JOSEPH FOWLER, Committed 27th November 1830, by The Rev. Charles Robert Ashfield, William Rickford Esq. John Lee aged 27, Esq. LL. D. and Robert Ludgate Esq. charged on the oath of Richard Ballad and others, with having *To be imprisoned in the* on the 26th November last, at the Parish of Waddesdon, in the said County, unlawfully, maliciously, *House of Correction to* and feloniously broken and destroyed a thrashing-machine, of the value of five pounds, of the goods of *hard Labour for Two* James Briggs. *Calendar Months.*

2. ROBERT HOPCRAFT, aged 28, ⎫ Committed 29th November 1830, by The Rev. Charles Robert Ashfield and The Rev. Alex-
3. EDMUND JARVIS, aged 33, ⎪ ander Lockhart, charged on the oath of John Rose and others, with having on the 26th
4. JOHN EVANS, aged 38, ⎬ November instant, riotously and unlawfully assembled with other persons to the number of
5. JOSEPH RIDGWAY, aged 20, ⎭ fifty, at the Parish of Waddesdon, in the said County, and unlawfully, maliciously, and *Hopcraft, Jarvis, and Evans,* feloniously broken and destroyed a certain machine called a winnowing-machine, of the value of ten *to be imprisoned in the* pounds, of the goods of Richard Hirons. *House of Correction to hard Labour for Six Weeks; Ridgway to be imprisoned until he procures one Surety in the sum of £10. to keep the Peace and be of good Behaviour for Two Years.*

6. JOSEPH HOLLAND, aged 27, ⎫ Committed 29th November 1830, by The Rev. Alexander Lockhart and The Rev. Charles
7. ISAAC DAVIS, aged 16, ⎬ Robert Ashfield, charged on the oath of James Collingridge and another, with having on
8. GEORGE HILLSDEN, aged 21, ⎭ 26th November instant, riotously and unlawfully assembled with other persons to the num- *All Acquitted.* ber of thirty, at the Parish of Waddesdon, in the said County, and unlawfully, maliciously, and feloni- ously broken and destroyed a certain machine called a chaff-cutting-machine, the property of William Rickford Esq.

9. PURCELL CORNELIUS TURNER, aged 40, ⎫ Committed 29th November 1830, by Robert Ludgate Esq. and The Rev.
10. STACEY JARVIS, aged 24, ⎪ Charles Robert Ashfield, charged by the oath of Richard Ballad, with having
11. JOHN NORMAN, aged 23, ⎪ on the 26th day of November last, at the Parish of Waddesdon, within the said
12. THOMAS SCOTT, aged 18, ⎬ County of Bucks, unlawfully, maliciously, and feloniously broken and destroyed
13. FRANCIS TACK, aged 28, ⎪ a certain thrashing-machine, of the value of five pounds, of the goods of
14. JOHN COPCUTT, aged 18, ⎪ the said Richard Ballad.
15. ELIJAH COWELL, aged 19, ⎭ *Turner, Jarvis, Tack, and Cowell, to be imprisoned in the House of Correction to hard Labour for Two Calendar Months; Norman, Scott, and Copcutt, convicted, and having entered into their own Recognizances in the sum of £30. each to appear when called on to receive the Judgment of the Court, and to keep the Peace and be of good Behaviour during the remainder of their Lives, Discharged.*

16. THOMAS HUGHES, alias WILLIAM HUGHES, Committed 29th November 1830, by The Rev. William Mussage Bradford aged 35, and John Augustus Sullivan Esq. charged on the oath of John Frith, with having at the Parish of *Convicted, and having en-* Beaconsfield, unlawfully assaulted and beaten the said John Frith, contrary to the form of the statute *tered into his own Recog-* in such case made; and that he also in the presence of the Magistrates, behaved in a riotous manner *nizance in the sum of £30.* and threatened the lives of the Magistrates, and attempted to rescue certain prisoners who were com- *to appear when called on* mitted for a riot, and were in charge of the said John Firth and the civil power. *to receive the Judgment of the Court, and to keep the Peace and be of good Behaviour for Two Years, Discharged.*

17. JOHN REYNOLDS, aged 29, ⎫
18. JOHN WALKER, aged 37, ⎪
19. JOSEPH PRIEST, aged 30, ⎪
20. JAMES BARTON, aged 23, ⎪ Committed 29th November 1830, by John Augustus Sullivan Esq. and The Rev. William
21. ROBERT CARY, alias ⎪ Mussage Bradford, charged on the oaths of William Lacey and others, with having on the 29th
  JOHN DELL, aged 23, ⎪ November last, unlawfully, riotously, and tumultuously assembled together, to the dis-
22. ALFRED SALTER, aged 19, ⎪ turbance of the public peace, at the mill and in the premises of Mr. William Robert Davis,
23. THOMAS FISHER, aged 26, ⎬ at the Parish of Chepping Wycombe, in the said County, and feloniously were present aiding,
24. RICHARD WEEDON, aged 41, ⎪ abetting, and assisting divers persons to as yet unknown, with the feloniously and unlawfully
25. JOHN SAWNEY, aged 54, ⎪ destroying certain machinery used in the manufacture of paper in the said mill, used in car-
26. JOHN EAST, aged 24, ⎪ rying on the trade or manufacture of a paper-maker, at the mill and on the premises of the
27. WILLIAM NIBBS, aged 24, ⎪ said William Robert Davis, at the Parish of Chepping Wycombe aforesaid, in the County of
28. JAMES STRETTON, aged 19, ⎪ Bucks aforesaid, against the form of the statute in that case made.
29. EDMUND BARTON, aged 24, ⎪
30. JAMES STONE, aged 24, ⎭ *Reynolds, Priest, James Barton, Salter, Fisher, Weedon, East, Nibbs, and Edmund Barton, Judgment of Death Recorded; Walker and Stretton, No True Bill, Discharged; Cary alias Dell, No Prosecution, Discharged; Sawney, Guilty, Death; Stone, Acquitted.*

A Calender of the prisoners in 1831, following the 1830 Paper Riots at High Wycombe.

ABOVE LEFT: Advertisement of John Rowell, a glass painter, 1732 and RIGHT: a sketch of John Rowell by J. Noller. BELOW LEFT: Tobacco advertisement of Warrell's, High Wycombe, c 1760 and RIGHT: Notice of a boot sale at Brook's, White Hart Street.

NOTICE.

POSITIVELY the LAST WEEK of BOOT SALE at BROOKS'S, White Hart Street, previous to opening at Queen Square. BOOTS at unheard-of prices to clear. It will pay you to purchase this week. Splendid line of Gents' 10/6 Boots going at 8/9, all in good condition. Football, Navvy, Men's, Women's, and Children's all at like reductions.

Note the Address -- White Hart Street.

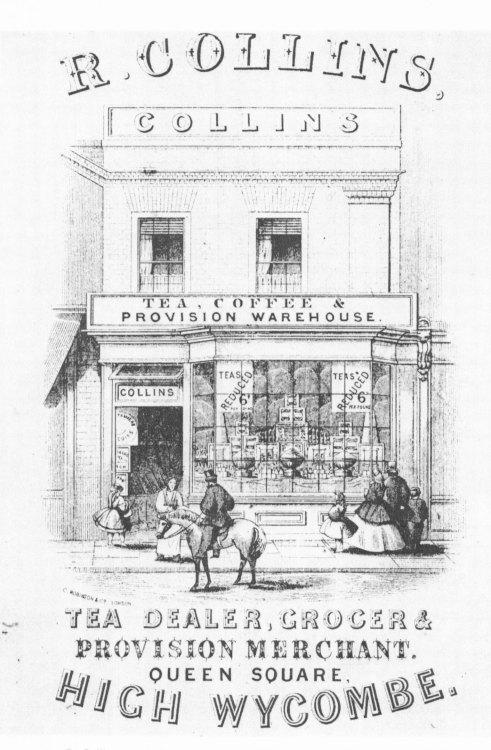

R. Collins, tea dealer, grocer and provisions merchant, Queen Square, High
Wycombe, c 1850.

Rather Dead Than Disloyal

From 1629 to 1640, Charles I governed the country without the help of Parliament. But Charles required money and resorted to a series of fines and taxes, often raised illegally. When a fleet was needed to fight the Dutch and ship-money levies were raised in 1634, 1635 and 1636 the public were outraged. The first levy was on the coastal counties, but that of 1636 was extended to cover the inland counties and so included Buckinghamshire. John Hampden and his party decided to resist payment. The case was argued before judges and decided in favour of the King. John Hampden, now a member of Parliament for Bucks, was hailed as the 'pilot that must steer this vessel through the tempest and rocks that threatened it'. On 3 January 1642 Charles ordered the arrest of five members of Parliament, including John Hampden and John Pym, an action which led to the Civil War.

The men of Bucks rallied to support Hampden and a thousand of them mounted and followed by others on foot rode to London to offer their services to Parliament. Hampden raised a foot regiment in Bucks and acted as its Colonel. Once the fighting started, Wycombe became an outpost of the Parliamentary forces against the nearby Royalist stronghold at Oxford. It was therefore fairly secure from attack as it was defended on the north and east by garrisons at Aylesbury, Wendover and Amersham, and on the south at Windsor Castle a Parliamentary force was in position under Col. Venn. Preparations were still in hand in October 1642 following the battle of Edgehill when it was learnt that Royalist troops under the King were at Oxford. Hampden went to Aylesbury to raise troops and arrange for supplies and men to come to Wycombe for a general rendezvous on 1 December 1642. On 5 December troops were engaged against the Royalists at Stokenchurch and on the next day, a large force of Royalist horse troops with some artillery was entrusted to Thomas Lord Wentworth. They skirted the town, entering from the North East down Hammersley Lane across the Wycombe Marsh and on to the Rye via Back Lane and Bassetsbury. The Parliamentary troops in Wycombe had not been idle, and defences, possibly in the area surrounding Horsenden Lane (now Queen Victoria Road) were thrown up by a small body of dragoons commanded by Captain Hayes. The story is taken up in a contemporary pamphlet: 'Lord Wentworth arrived neere the said forces...where he sounded his trumpets and made a glorious shew upon the tops of two great hills thinkeing the day to be his owne, for he had information that the forces which lay there about, did not amount to above foure or five thousand of them and had set then in two vayllyes one the left side of Wickham, carrying their colours low, and every man traylling his Pike becase the enemy should not discry then, and gave them strict charge that everyman should be silent. When they see the enemy advance towards Wickham they should fall on so soone as they heard the ordnance fire, which command they very diligently observed. No sooner had the ordnance discharged but they fell on fighting with extraordinary courage and much policy which when the enemy seing were amazed to see such a company behind them and another before them. The ordnances played very fast, and the Commander of the volunteers shewd very discretion, so that for the space of foure houres they fought very valiantly, till at last the enemy retreated leaving behind them at least nine hundred of their confederates [Royalists] slaine and maymed in the filed, the young Lord Wentworth being dangerously wounded all this done with loose of three hunden men [Parliamentary]forces '.

The position of Wycombe was important as a military town, but it seems that not all its residents were loyal to the Parliamentary cause. In the Journal of Sir Samuel Luke we read 'The King's forces have a supply of all grocery wares and other commodityes by carriers which pritent at the courts of guard at London they have them out for the Parliments use' but that 'all commodityes which the Cavileers want are sent from London to Wickham under Wickham mens names, and soe sent in the night to Oxford by waggons loades at a tyme'.

The Royalists made several attacks on Wycombe, and Sir Samuel Luke writes on May 1643 'On Monday last an ensign went out of Oxford privately with an intent to sett fire to West Wickham and High Wickham, but was prevented by a coachman whoe overheard his designs and caused him to bee apprehended'. But on 24 June Col Sir John Urry made a more strategic attack. Accompanied by a number of foot soldiers, he proceeded to Stokenchurch where they spent the night. The next morning, after sacking Chinnor and Postcombe, they moved towards Wycombe on the Marlow ridge and coming down into Wycombe on the old Marlow Road they attacked the Parliamentary Garrison which was on the site of Wycombe Abbey grounds. Reports vary as to the result, with one giving the Royalists a sweeping victory, and others reporting that the Parliamentary troops gave way quickly and withdrew towards Beaconsfield. Col Urry and his troops left Wycombe shortly after, and the Parliamentary troops returned to the Town. So the attacks continued. On 12 Dec 1643 thirty Cavaliers plundered houses in Wycombe and carried away four of the townsmen. The Mayor's wife followed them to get back her goods, but they made her prisoner also and demanded a ransom of £45. It seems unlikely that they got this money, for in January 1644 the Cavaliers threatened to plunder and burn 'the town of Wickham if they bring not in 40 Li [£40] tomorrow, when they have assessed them to pay'.

In 1644 Sir Richard Browne, who was later to become the Member of Parliament for Wycombe, made the town his Headquarters. During the Civil War, life had continued much as normal in the Borough, and although many deaths are mentioned in connection with local skirmishes, parish registers show few burials to substantiate the losses. As the Borough was in debt, possibly due to the interruption of the Market and the loss of market tolls, attempts were made in 1646 to allot to the poor only half the tolls collected by the Mayor. In September 1649 this caused a riot on Market Day, with two hundred people agitating against a decision to reduce or even withhold the payment of any toll corn to the poor. Rioters seized grain from the farmers, and troops were brought in to suppress the mob.

On Michaelmas 1650, Stephen Bates was made Mayor and the previous Mayor invalidated the election and turned Bates and his supporters out of the Guildhall. This decision was reversed by the Council of State, and Stephen Bates, described as 'a discreet, religious person, nominated by the well affected of the town' was reinstated. Five years later in November 1655, another petition reached the Council of State from the townspeople complaining that they were excluded from the Corporation and that unfit persons were admitted to its ranks by the Mayor, Justices and Common Council. This petition was upheld and Col Tobias Bridge was sent down to Wycombe. His report included the need for a new Charter and the Borough had to borrow £50 to pay for it. Officials who had to leave following his visit included Alderman Nicholas Bradshaw, Bailiff Thomas Sedgewick, John Bowlter the Town Clerk and George Howdeats, Sergeant-at-Mace.

The King surrendered to the Scots at Newark and they in turn surrendered him to the English Parliament for a payment of £200,000 down and £200,000 later. Due to considerable friction within the army, Parliament sent representatives to High Wycombe on 1 July 1647 to negotiate with the Army the Impeachment of the King in what is known as 'The Treaty of Wycombe'. Charles was offered the following conditions: firstly that Parliament was to control the Militia, Navy and Offices of State for ten years; secondly that religious toleration was to be extended to all sects, except the Roman Catholics; thirdly that the duration of Parliament should be limited to two years and the seats fairly represented; lastly that this settlement would include all Charles' army and politicians with the exception of five close advisers. Charles refused these conditions and so went to trial.

The people of High Wycombe saw him on his way, for the Ledger Book records that 'King Charles marched through this town...towarde Woborne in Bedforshire...and afterwards was beheaded at Whitehall upon the 30th day of January 1648 to the ppetuall infamy of the English Nation'. Among his judges was Adrian Scrope, who had been one of the candidates at a previous Wycombe Parliamentary election, and Thomas Scott, who was Member of Parliament for the Borough 1654-59. Both were executed in October 1660 as regicides and Scott asked for his tombstone to have the simple legend 'Here lies Thomas Scott, one of the King's Judges'. Another of the regicides who signed the King's death warrant was Sir Hardress Waller who managed to avoid execution. He was the father of Elizabeth Waller who married Sir William Petty, and was mother of Charles, 1st Lord Shelburne of Wycombe Abbey.

In May 1660 King Charles II landed at Dover and on the same day the Mayor, the

Bailiffs, six Aldermen and thirty-two Burgesses resigned their offices, and on 30 May Richard Nelson was appointed Mayor. The pages in the Ledger Book which recorded Tobias Bridge's judgement regarding the Mayoralty and the new Charter were cut out and the words 'Now we have a King again' written in the margin.

The Charter of Cromwell, which had cost the Borough in all £150, was burnt in front of the Guildhall, and the action proudly recorded in the Ledger Book: 'This was the charter which the Rumpers did gain from that grand Rebel Oliver'. A new Charter was obtained from Charles II in November 1663 shortly after he visited High Wycombe in September of that year. 'King Charles the Second with his Queen, Katherine, the Duke of York and his Duchess and Prince Rupert, the Duke of Monmouth and many others of the Nobility did lodge in Wickcombe the 30th Day of September in the yeare 1663…the King did go out to Town between v and vi of the clock next morning and was at His Palace at Whitehall before 9 of the clocke in the morning. The King was lodged with his Queen at the Catherine Wheel'. The new charter confirmed the rights and privileges of previous Charters and constituted Nicholas Bradshaw, evicted by Cromwell's Charter, as an Alderman once again. Bradwell was appointed Mayor for the fourth time in 1672 when he must have been advanced in age, for in the midst of his inaugural banquet he suddenly died.

Another Royalist, Richard Lucas, kept the Red Lion, and was an alderman for twenty six years and three times Mayor. In 1670 he issued a trade token which is inscribed on one side 'Richard Lucas of Wickham, Red Lion L,R,D, 1670' and on the reverse the brave slogan 'Rather dead than disloyal'. But the years of the Restoration were also sad ones for the parishioners. In 1665, out of 149 deaths, 96 were from the plague, and in 1666 the death toll from the plague was 101. But that year was the end of the pestilence, and the decade was the end of the Commonwealth and of the Civil War, for, in the words in the High Wycombe Borough Ledger Book: 'Wee have a King come now, God by praysed'.

The impeachment of the five MPs, written by Charles I.

Gentlemen

The army is now at North Hampton mouing euvry day nra rer to you. if you dysband not wee may be a mutuall succour each to other but if you dysperse you make your selues & yⁿ country a pray you shall hear daily frō

North Hampt octob· 31

Yoʳ seruant
Hampden

For my noble frend. Colonell Bulfrod Captaine Grenfield Captaine Tyrrell Captaine Weſt or any of them

John Hampden's letter from the army at North Hampton, with INSET: a portrait of Hampden

The Kings party haveing information of these proceedings, the Lord *wentworth*, Sonne to the late deceased Earle of *Straford*, with about five thousand horse advanced toward the said forces at *Wickham* and *Alsbury* in *buckinghamshire*, where they lay billited, but our forces having information of their comming, with all the speed that they possibly could make, they began to make breast-workes, and made two halfe Moones where they had planted seven Peeces of ordnance haveing received them from his Excellence and upon the sixt of this month the Lord *Wentworth* arived neere the said forces at *alsbury* and *VVickham* where he sounded his trumpets and made a glorious shew upon the tops of two great hils thinkeing the day to be his owne, for he had information that the forces which lay there about, did not a-mount to above, foure or five thousand and indeed well might he receive this newes, for one Captaine *Hayes*, which commanded the greatest part of these forces, had drawn out neare upon foure thousand of them and had set them in two vayllyes one the left side of *VVickham*, carrying their Colours low, and

5 3   (A   every

Glorious and Happy Victory: part of a pamphlet published following the battle of High Wycombe, and INSET: portrait of Richard Browne, M.P. of Chepping Wycombe in 1640.

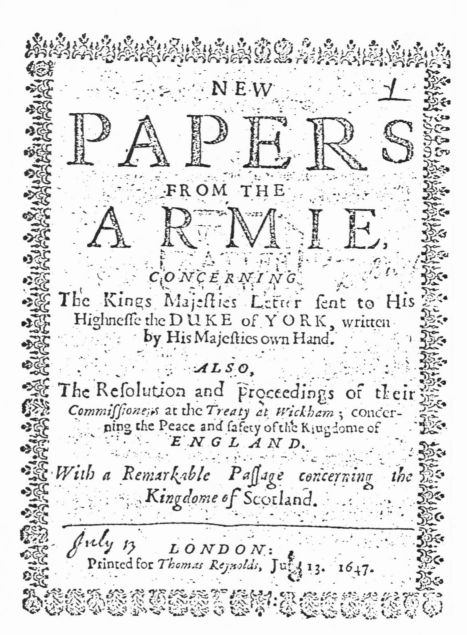

NEW PAPERS
FROM THE
ARMIE,

CONCERNING

The Kings Majesties Letter sent to His
Highnesse the DUKE of YORK, written
by His Majesties own Hand.

ALSO,

The Resolution and Proceedings of their
Commissioners at the *Treaty at Wickham*; concerning the Peace and safety of the Kingdome of
ENGLAND.

With a Remarkable Passage concerning the
Kingdome of Scotland.

July 13   LONDON:
Printed for *Thomas Reynolds*, July 13. 1647.

Part of *New Papers from the Armie,* 1647, which included the Treaty of
Wickham.

ABOVE LEFT: Hannah Ball's signature on a lease with the Borough, 1768. RIGHT: The town drum, which was beaton loudly to drown the sound of the services Wesley was taking. BELOW: A letter from Wesley to Hannah Ball in 1779, in sympathy on her mother's death, and exhorting her to build a new chapel, with INSET: a portrait of John Wesley in 1742, by J.M. Williams.

Freedom of Conscience

The official position of the High Wycombe Borough on freedom of religion is summed up fairly clearly in the oath sworn by the Town Clerk and others when taking office in 1717. 'I do sweare that I doe from my heart abhor and detest and abjure as impious and hereticall that Damnable doctrine and position that Princes excommunicated or deprived by the Popes or any authority of the See of Rome may be deposed or murthered by their subjects or any other whatsoever'.

Despite this official attitude, there has been a tradition of non-conformity stretching back to the Lollards, and while Amersham and Chesham were well known for their Lollard sympathies, Wycombe men were involved from the 15th century. Among those arrested in London in St Giles Field in 1414 and charged with treason and imprisoned was John Langacre, a mercer of Wycombe and with others pardoned were Richard Norton alias Spicer of Wycombe, a cooper, Thomas Sebeley, a fletcher of Wycombe Heath, and a fishmonger of London called John Child who had some form of business in this town. In 1464 an examination was held in Wycombe Church of the heretics. Richard Benett of High Wycombe was the first to ajbure his errors, and on 14 June another seven were also questioned before the Bishop of Lincoln with three local men recanting. A couple of months later on 1 October another eleven heretics from High Wycombe, Turville, Great Marlow and Hughenden recanted.

A hundred years later, South Bucks was still well known for its non-conformity and the Bishop of Lincoln, John Longland, was equally notorious from 1521 for his persecution of heretics. Longland was so disliked and feared that in 1539 he was accused by two priests and twenty-four men of Wycombe for failing to pray for the King and not speaking against the 'Bishop of Rome'. One of the leaders of this group was John Raunce, Bailiff of Bassetsbury 1532-36. Four years later his son, Robert Raunce, broke into the University Church of St Mary and stole chalices and other Church items from the Chapel of John Longland, but he was pardoned in 1545. John Raunce eventually became Mayor of Wycombe in 1552.

Not everyone was against the traditional Church, for when the images and relics were removed from the Church of All Saints in the Reign of Edward VI, John Blisse protested to the extent of being imprisoned in the Fleet in London, and he was then brought back to Wycombe to confess his sins in public. The number of religious sects in Wycombe had given it the derisive name of 'a holy towne'. These sects thrived in

Wycombe until the passsing of the Conventicle Act of 1664 which prohibited assemblies for religious services except in the parish church. Most of these non-conformists would have been Presbyterians or Baptists, but other more extreme groups such as Levellers who joined the new sect of Quakers, obtained no protection under either Protectorate or Restoration. Wycombe adherents included the families of Steevens, Ball and Littleboy and the formidable Dr John Raunce, whose great-grandfather had led the petition against the Bishop of Lincoln in 1539. His house may have been in Crendon Lane, for he was granted a licence for a meeting house there in 1689. But during the Commonwealth period the monthly meetings of the group took place in Raunce's house or that of Jeremiah Steevens in the White House in High Street. Thomas Ellwood came to Wycombe in 1659 but he found himself at odds with John Raunce who wrote a pamphlet 'News from Wickham' attacking his views. This caused a division of the Friends. Soon after the Conventicle Act was passed, John Raunce's home was raided on the Sunday and seven Quakers were charged with meeting 'under the pretence of religious worship', and sentenced to imprisonment in the 'House of Correction' in Frogmore, which was termed by them 'a loathsome dungeon'. Raunce himself was not arrested but his turn came at Amersham when he was imprisoned for a month in 1671 and Thomas Ellwood was imprisoned in Wycombe for three months in 1666.

Dissent was so strong in the Commonwealth period, that it left many as outcasts after the Restoration. Samuel Guy had been an Alderman in 1656 and Mayor in 1657 when he was described in the Ledger Books as 'This Guy was a forward man for the Rumper's cause' and he was one of the independents at whose house a group 'mostly of the middle and meaner sort met'. Following the Declaration of Indulgence in 1672, licences were granted to Rev George Swinnock, MA and to congregations of Baptists, Presbyterians and Independents. About 1711 a note by Browne Willis records 'there are no Papists here, but five meeting houses of dissenters'. The Act of Toleration enabled them to build chapels and the Independents built a chapel in Crendon Lane in 1714 while across the lane an old barn had served the Quakers for some years. The Baptists had a cottage adapted as a chapel, purchased in 1709 partly from money left by James Raunce.

On 12 November 1739, John Wesley rode into Wycombe, and standing in the market place preached on the parable of the 'Pharisee and the Publican'. He and his followers were already called Methodists, although it was not until 1740 that the Methodist Society was formed. This was the first of over thirty visits he made between 1739 and 1789 during which time Wesley got to know Hannah Ball (1733-1792) whose family lived in a house in Queen Square. Their first contact was when he preached on the text 'O woman, great is thy faith; be it unto thee even as thou wilt'. Hannah Ball said later, 'I felt as if a tongue of fire sat upon my heart, healing the wound that sin had made'. Wesley wrote of her that she had 'a peculiar love for children and a talent for assisting them'. In 1769 she conceived the idea of instructing children on Sundays, instituting a small class at the Parish Church. The actual transfer from the Anglican Church to Methodism took place gradually, and in 1779, financed by James Batting but inspired by Hannah Ball, the local Methodists built their Chapel in St Mary Street.

When Wesley visited the group in 1777, he preached in a house next door to that owned by John Stone James, who was known to be hostile to the non-conformists. John Wesley wrote of his visit in his diary 'Good Mr James procured a drummer to beat his drum at the window of the preaching house. I only prayed and sung in turn from six to seven'. So this could be the reason why he later wrote to Hannah Ball regarding a new meeting house. 'I will give you a plan of a building myself and employ who you please to build.' The new chapel was opened by Wesley before a 'crowded and genteel audience' and he preached on the text 'We preach Christ Crucified'.

Hannah's own ministry among the children also progressed and she and her sister Ann are believed to be the first Sunday School teachers, even before Robert Raikes of Gloucester who started one in 1780, and was long considered the originator. Hannah Ball wished to spend her time 'ministering to them that shall be heirs to salvation' and she additionally formed a Monday class who, according to a letter she wrote to Wesley 'are a wild little company but seem willing to be instructed'. In 1788 her health failed and she found it difficult to get about, and only wished to 'go home, like a ship richly laden'. She died in 1792. In his last letter to her, Wesley reminded her to 'Look up my dear friend, the prize is before us, we are on the point of parting no more. In time and eternity you will be united with your ever affectionate brother, John Wesley'. She was buried in the family tomb in Stokenchurch graveyard.

To escape the rigid religious laws and regulations of the 16th and 17th centuries, the dissidents either conformed, or emigrated to the new colonies in America. Some adventurers went from profit motives rather than religious conviction, and among these was Armagil Waad or Wade (d1568) who was elected Member of Parliament for Wycombe in 1547. His tombstone in Hampstead Church rather grandly calls him the 'English Columbus' but while this is an exaggerated claim, he was early in the field, and joined Hore's voyage to North America in April 1536. They visited Cape Breton, Newfoundland and Penguin Island, returning to England in October the same year. He remained the representative of Chepping Wycombe until the accession of Queen Mary in 1553. This voyage was almost a century before the Mayflower reached America in 1620, and contrary to general belief, there were English colonists on that continent when the Pilgrim Fathers landed. On 27 May 1615, the Wycombe Borough Council Ledger book recorded the names of the 'adventurers for Virgina'; those who ventured sums of money in the lottery made for the new settlement. The amounts varied, with Robert Kempe, Gent. subscribing 40s, John Raunce 20s; other amounts varied from 10s to 13s 4d while shares were also purchased for a number of children at 5s each including those for Thomas Welles, son of John. In April 1638 Nicholas Bradshaw as Overseer of the poor, paid 20s for orphan Oxlade's passage to Virginia as an apprentice.

The interest of the Welles family in America crops up later when Marjory Welles,

EFT: The Bird-In-Hand Sunday School, opened in
enry Keen. CENTRE: White Hart Street Chapel,
875 and designed by Arthur Vernon, and RIGHT:
ch, Crendon Street, built 1889-97, also designed by
ELOW LEFT: The door of the Friends Meeting
ndon Street, in 1922 and RIGHT: Trinity Chapel
ng the River Wye at Pann Mill, erected in 1850.

daughter of Thomas Welles, (Mayor of Wycombe 1607 and 1637) married John Lane of Hughenden. Their son founded the Lane family which provided Maryland with a number of its Governors, and another member of the family was Sir Ralph Lane, the first Governor of Virginia. Thomas Welles had sold his manors of Temple Wycombe and Windsor to the Quaker John Raunce in 1609, and Raunce in turn sold them to Richard Archdale in 1628. His grandson was John Archdale (b 1642)who became one of George Fox's followers and he is believed also to have owned a house in Crendon Street. In 1664 he set out for America with Ferdinando Georges, his brother-in-law, to establish the claim of the Georges family to the Governorship of territories in the State of Maine. They proved successful and John Archdale became Governor of North Carolina. He remained in America until 1697 when he returned to High Wycombe, and was elected the following year as Parliamentary Member for the Borough. However, as he was a professed Quaker, he was debarred from taking up his seat, and was replaced by his only son Thomas, who in 1700 sold his estates, including Loakes Manor, to Lord Shelburne.

The original building of the Union Baptist Church, Easton Street, opened in
1845 and destroyed by fire in 1908.

Havenfield,
High Wycombe.
Feb 1908

Dear Sir,

I am desired by the Pastor & deacons of Union Baptist Chapel to request you to convey to the Volunteer Fire Brigade under your command our grateful appreciation and that of our Church of the very efficient prompt and skilful services of the Brigade in their efforts in extinguishing the fire at the Chapel —

It was doubtless due to these services that the School room was saved and further devastation ~~~~~ prevented

Please assure the Brigade of our gratitude

Yours faithfully
[signature]

Mr W. H. Butler.
Captain of Fire Brigade.

ABOVE: Letter of thanks from the Pastor and Deacons of Union Baptist Chapel, 1908. BELOW: Frogmore House in 1903, later demolished to become the site of the Salvation Army citadel.

ABOVE: The Priory, Castle Street, the site of the residence of the Wellesbourne family who sent three members to Parliament to represent Chepping Wycombe, with INSET: a portrait of the Earl of Shelburne, by Joshua Reynolds. RIGHT: Benjamin Franklin, the American diplomat and friend of Sir Francis Dashwood and BELOW: Wycombe Abbey, home of the Shelburne and Carington families, rebuilt by James Wyatt in 1795.

Lords and Commons

Wycombe has been represented in Parliament since 1298, for when John La Lude was elected to attend Parliament in 1300, it was to replace Stephen Ayot 'who was at the last Parliament' and Thomas Le Tailleur 'the other Burgess of Wycombe who came to the last Parliament' which took place in 1298. Most of our early representatives were local Burgesses and Edmundde Haveringdon, William Le Cassiere and Benedict Le Cassiere, who were in Parliament between 1309 and 1323, were local butchers. But it soon became the custom to elect a more prominent citizen to this responsible position, and who better than a senior Burgess or a past mayor? Of the twenty three Burgesses who were elected Mayor between 1309 and 1476, sixteen had previously, or later served in Parliament, with several sitting on more than one occasion. The Burgesses paid them 2s a day (compared to the 4d earned by workmen at Bassetsbury Manor), and the Parliament of 1376 cost the Borough over £15. This payment ceased following a writ of Parliament in 1510, for the Ledger Book reports 'and further that the said George and Richard will not receive any fee of the aforesaid Borough for their stipends for the business above.'

Among 15th century members was John Wellesbourne, who sat in Parliament between 1425 and 1453, and his son was our representative from 1447-1449, while his son Thomas Wellesbourne was elected in 1476. Another family who represented the Borough at the same time was that of the Fowlers of Rycote, Oxon. William Fowler was MP in 1431-2, his younger son Thomas Fowler followed him and was elected in 1495. Thomas's elder brother, Richard Fowler sat as member for Bucks in 1467-8 and in 1472 became Chancellor of the Exchequer, and Governor of the infant Prince of Wales in 1473, murdered in the Tower of London in 1477.

In the 16th century, parliamentarians were often elected through the strong influences within the Borough, and in the reign of Queen Mary, Henry Peckham was our member, and was supported by local personalities such as his father Sir Edmund Peckham, Sir William Windsor and Sir William Dormer in proclaiming Mary as Queen. However Henry was soon involved in an attempt to de-throne Queen Mary and make Elizabeth queen, so bringing in a Protestant regime, but he came under suspicion and was hanged on Tower Hill 7 May 1556. In 1594 the Borough ruled that only Burgesses residing in the Borough could elect or be elected as Mayor or Member of Parliament. In not all cases did the election go according to plan, or even according to law. In the election of 1721-2 Lord Shelburne decided to offer himself for the Wycombe seat in Parliament in which other contestants were the Hon Charles Egerton and Henry Waller of Hall Barn, Beaconsfield. The Mayor at that time, Edward Bedder decided to support Henry Waller and so created eighty three new Burgesses with the consent of the majority of the Aldermen to enable Waller to be elected. Lord Shelburne was so enraged that he managed to overthrow the Mayor in August and put one of his own party in office.

Waller had to defend his seat again in February 1722, but as the new Mayor, Richard Shrimpton favoured Shelburne's candidate, the Hon Charles Collyear, 'above seventy honorary Freemen scattered abroad in all parts of the Kingdom' were made who also favoured Collyear. Both parties were ready for trouble this time, and the Town Chamberlain early on the day of the election opened the Town Hall to allow Henry Waller and his supporters to crowd in and fill the Hall and so gain advantage. At half past two, when the poll was due to open, Mayor Richard Shrimpton, with a noise of 'drums, kettledrums, trumpets, Hautboys and other Warlike Appearence' came on the scene with the other candidate, and after a token attempt to get into the Town Hall adjourned to The George Inn on the other side of the street, where he held the election, declaring Collyear the winner by 49 votes to 2 votes.

There was an immediate objection on the part of Henry Waller and, as the *St James Evening Post* of 19 March 1725 states: 'Richard Shrimpton, Mayor of Chipping Wycombe in the County of Bucks was committed to Newgate on Thursday last on account of some very foul practices in the late elections of a Member of Parliament for the said Borough'. On 17 March, by order of the House, Collyear's name was erased and that of Henry Waller inserted, so taking up his position and acting in Parliament until 1730 when Edmund Waller and Edmund Waller jnr took over.

The drums and music mentioned above were an integral part of the local elections as the list of expenses shows; also a considerable amount of direct or indirect bribery was involved. In June 1754, a newssheet reported that Lord Shelburne gave £1,000 to the town 'to be disposed of as the inhabitants think proper' adding the sardonic comment 'That is not bribery!'

A chair, painted up and re-upholstered, was used to carry the successful candidate around the town; 12 chair carriers were involved. Another election custom concerns a large wooden key about five feet long, now in the local museum and donated by P.C. Raffety in 1932. This is known as the Key of the Borough and was first used in the 1841 election, and until that of 1883, after which the Wycombe Division was formed. Its existence was due to the rivalry between the town and Abbey in securing Parliamentary representatives of the Borough. When the Town candidate was successful, the key, garlanded with flowers, headed a joyful procession in celebration of the result. When the Abbey nominee proved successful at the poll, the key was harnessed to the tail of a donkey. Wycombe was also one of the Chiltern Hundreds which in ancient days were so much a haunt for robbers and outlaws that the duty of a Steward was necessary to keep travellers safe. Although the need for this service had long disappeared by the 18th century, the Office of Steward with a nominal salary had not been abolished and it was a convenient subterfuge to adopt when a member wished to resign from Parliament. A clause of the Act of Settlement 1700 disqualified any member from holding an office of profit under the Crown unless re-elected, but it was not until 1751 that the first application for the Chilterns was applied for, and since then this has been common practice.

The 1st Lord Shelburne purchased the Manor of Loakes, Temple Wycombe and Windsor or Chapel Fee from Thomas Archdale in 1700, and he, and later his successor, the 3rd Lord Shelburne set about to improve his Wycombe Estate. The grounds of Loakes Park were laid out with ornamental walks and cages were erected for wild animals. While Lord Shelburne was Colonial Secretary, Lord Sandwich made an offer of a 'wild beast' in a letter of 1763, and Lady Shelburne in her diary mentioned on Christmas Day 1768 a 'poor wild man of the wood' dying in the night due to the intense cold. Shelburne also considerably enlarged and improved the house under the direction of the architect James Wyatt in 1795 and it then became known as Wycombe Abbey. The 1st Lord Shelburne died in 1751 and the Earldom eventually rested on John Fitzmaurice, provided he took the family name of Petty. John 2nd Earl of Shelburne was created Baron Wycombe in May 1760 but died a year later in 1761. He was succeeded by William, 3rd Earl who had represented the Borough in Parliament when his father moved to the House of Lords. Lord Shelburne served in several important offices of State under successive Prime Ministers and became Prime Minister himself in 1783. He was interested in extending his estates and in 1764 obtained the lease of lands adjoining Horsenden Lane (now Queen Victoria Road) for 99 years, and so enclosed it, bringing his entrance drive right up to the High Street. Here he built a stone archway known as the Rupert Gates which stood in front of the present Library Gardens between the traffic lights and the offices in High Street. In his position as a senior minister and then as Premier, the Abbey became the centre of a civilised and cultured circle. Visitors included Dr Johnson, Edmund Burke, Joshua Reynolds, John Boswell, Oliver Goldsmith and the actor Garrick, Benjamin Franklin, John Wesley, and the scientist Dr Priestley who first demonstrated the existence of oxygen, and whose Wedgewood likeness is in the local museum, presented by his descendant, Dr Priestley of Terriers House.

Sir Francis Dashwood was also in Parliament, until elevated to the House of Lords. In 1762, when the Earl of Bute was Prime Minister, Sir Francis was Chancellor of the Exchequer but his first budget was far from a success, and Dashwood admitted to 'a profound aversion to mathematics all my life. I am quite incapable of doing any sum which contains more than five figures'. He became Lord le Despencer in 1763, and in Pitt's ministry was made Postmaster General. His claim to fame probably lies in his connection with the Hell-fire Club:

> 'Oh to the Club, the scene of savage joys,
> The school of coarse good fellowships and noise.' (Cowper)

This group, probably formed about 1746, became the 'Knights of Saint Francis' in

1755 with the members calling themselves monks and the final meeting place being Medmenham Abbey on the banks of the Thames. Within the Club were many prominent figures, and although wining and dining seems to have been the chief pursuit, a certain amount of wenching and religious or demonic ceremonies brought its reputation into bad odour, and it died out with Sir Francis's own death in 1781. West Wycombe Park was remodelled by Sir Francis about 1750 and completed by 1780. Near to the house, and halfway down the hill is the entrance to the Hell-Fire Caves. These were excavated to provide chalk for the road between West Wycombe and High Wycombe, and they extend a quarter of a mile into the chalk hill, going to a depth of 300 feet below the surface. The Dashwood family still had an interest in Parliament, and in the 1790 elections at Wycombe, John Dashwood-King, the son of Sir Francis Dashwood's stepbrother, was a candidate, receiving a good number of votes, but not sufficient to unseat the Earl of Wycombe or his fellow candidate who was the prominent naval man Sir John Jervis. John Dashwood-King was elected in 1796 and held his seat until 1831. George H. Dashwod was elected in 1841 and he found himself, like Lord Shelburne earlier, involved in the poor finances of the Borough and provided money for the renovation of the Guildhall in 1859.

In the early years of the 19th century, a bizarre figure arrived in the person of Benjamin Disraeli. The government of Lord Wellington had fallen and Grey and the Whigs were in power with an interest in parliamentary reform. In 1831 a petition in favour of the reform of the Parliamentary representation of the Borough of High Wycombe was signed by most of the householders and on 4 June 1832 the Lords passed the Reform Bill with the town cheering the result. The time had come for Sir Thomas Baring to retire from the seat at Wycombe, and this vacancy was sought by the young author Disraeli, whose father lived at Bradenham. Announcing himself a radical, Disraeli stated 'I am still a reformer, but shall destroy the foreign policy of the Grey Faction' and his slogan in Wycombe was 'Grey and Reform versus Disraeli and the People'.

The Government was worried at the outcome of the Wycombe by-election and Col Grey, Lord Grey's son was brought down as the government candidate. Disraeli attempted to gain support among the influential persons in the town, writing to T.G.Tatum 'You may perhaps not be unaware that it is my intention to offer myself as a Representative for this Boro'. In so doing I come forward on principles the most decidedly liberal, and supported by the sanction of our public men ... I am desirous of submitting their comments to yourself as the most influential, the most able and most sincere reformer in Wycombe ...'

Unfortunately for Disraeli, another letter had already reached Mr Tatum with a House of Commons heading which merely noted 'I hope that you and our other friends at High Wycombe ... will exert themselves to support Col Grey on his election ... and I need not say what is due to Lord Grey's son - I shall be glad to hear of his triumphant reception'.

In the lead-up to the election, Disraeli made his famous comments while standing on the portico of the Red Lion 'When the poll is declared, my opponent will be there [pointing to the Lion's tail] and I shall be here' (pointing to the lion's head). In the final result Col Grey polled 20 votes and Disraeli 12 votes. When he tried again in the General Election of October 1832 with a much greater franchise, Grey polled 140 and Disraeli 119. Following the second Reform Bill, the Borough returned only one candidate, and in 1884 it lost its representation and became part of a larger Wycombe Division.

The politics of Wycombe were still influenced strongly by the Abbey, with Carington, who now owned the property, playing an active part in local politics at both parliamentary and local council levels.

Disraeli made his way into Parliament without the help of Wycombe, and achieved the position of Prime Minister and confidant of the Queen. It was Victoria who honoured the borough when she came on 15 December 1877 to see her Premier at his home, Hughenden Manor. Flags and banners were displayed and triumphal arches erected, one constructed of chairs. The Queen was met at the station by Benjamin Disraeli, and presented with a Loyal Address by the Mayor.

Lord and Lady Carington with Viscount Wendover in their Coronation robes, 1902.

ABOVE: The Rupert Gates in High Street 1898, with the brewery on the extreme right. and BELOW: the Gates in 1891 when they were rebuilt at the entrance to Daws hill, by workmen of Hull, Loosely and Pearce Ltd.

DIZZEY & THE WYCOMBE LION,

WHO HAS LOST HIS HEAD,

Where Mr. Disraeli made his Maiden Speech to the Electors of Wycombe in 1831.

In Wycombe town a Lion stood,
  Where Dizzey made a speech,
Upon a well-built portico,
  Out of the peoples' reach.

Then Dizzey pitched into the Whigs,
  With Rads on both his sides;
The Tories looked, and gaped, and sighed,
  While *Carter tanned their hides.

The Lion, too, he looked affright,
  To hear the speech he made,
A Radical he was outright,
  But how things change and fade ! !

Then Dizzey said, "Now, Charley Grey,
  Just go a-head and rail,
I—have got the Lion's head,
  I—leave to you his tail."

The Radicals cried out, hurrah,
  Disraeli, Disraeli, for ever;
He is the man for us my boys,
  We'll put Grey in the river.

But now the Lion's head is gone,
  His old tail still remains,
And Dizzey's prospects are not bright;
  His heart is full of pains.

* Chairman of Mr. D.'s Committee.

LEFT: Benjamin Disraeli as the Elder Statesman, and RIGHT: Dizzey and the Wycombe Lion.

ABOVE: Queen Victoria and Lord Beaconsfield at High Wycombe Railway Station, December 1877. BELOW: The Borough Key in use from 1841-1883, presented by P.C. Raffety in 1932.

Wye, Warriors and Wine

Henry Kingston, writing in 1848, pictured Wycombe: 'The beechclad hills of Bucks .... encompass not a more picturesque valley that it does the place where stands my Native Town. Sequestered little spot! Adorned by nature with many delightful varieties of Hill and dale, it seems to afford security for retirement; and those who love to watch the sparkling brook and gaze with delight on the verdure and fertility of the surrounding pasture, ... may dwell for a time in Wycombe, and ''babble o' green fields''.'

Certainly the town was much smaller then, for it consisted chiefly of the High Street which extended to Pann Mill in the East, of Crendon Lane to the corner of the present Castle Street, and into St Mary Street as far as the British Legion Hall site, into Frogmore to Temple Farm: Benjamin Road, and along West Wycombe Road as far as Bridge Street. Within this area a number of houses dating from the 18th century still survive, although we must look above the shop fronts to see them. Most of the High Street on either side consisted of large houses or business premises at the front overlooking the street, with numerous archways leading to yards in which other craftsmen and traders worked and lived in sheds, stables and upper rooms. From the south side of the street, the gardens led almost down to the River Wye, taking over the meadows which originally lay there, while to the north of the northern side of High Street the ends of the long gardens met the grounds of Vicarage Farm and Castle Hill. Here was the dell in which the boxing matches took place, and there was no road leading from the Vicarage to Crendon Lane as now. Just about where the railway lies now were the gates of the town which were closed at dusk, and woe betide any stranger who wandered the town at night, as he would almost certainly end up in the prison below the Old Guildhall. Castle Hill House itself overlooked the town and was owned in 1883 by Robert Nash, a lawyer who was Town Clerk and Clerk to the Beaconsfield and Stokenchurch Turnpike Trust. Soon after it was purchased, Nash extended the building. The estate included the present Priory Road and Priory Avenue, and extended to Amersham Road down to what is now the public house called 'Flint Cottage'. This originally had a coach house and stables, and was most probably the Lodge at the entrance to the drive of Castle Hill House. Unfortunately when the Maidenhead to Wycombe Railway line was extended to Thame in 1862, the railway cut through the estate, depriving it of much of the lower slopes of the grounds. After

Robert Nash died, it was purchased by the Carington Estate and leased to John Rumsey, and by 1869 the occupier was John Edwards who was Treasurer of the National schools in High Wycombe. By the end of the 19th century it had been sold to James George Peace and in 1908 to Arthur J. Clarke, Town Clerk of High Wycombe. His son Roland P. Clarke, who was Mayor in 1936-7 and 1953-4 sold the property to the Borough in 1962 when it became the Museum.

Back down the valley into Frogmore, the waste land in the centre had been fenced off to act as the Borough Pound for stray animals; however, in 1737 the Town Chamberlain was directed to remove the fencing and arrange for an ornamental piece of water to be dug, surrounded by trees. The pound formerly at the east end of the Rye in Pound Mead, was situated in Frogmore in 1686. The Hogmarket, the area outside the churchyard gates in High Street, in a lease of 1686 was recorded as 'now or late used as a pound'. The meadows beyond Frogmore were known as Templemede and Temple More or as the 'great meadows of the Templars' and were a favourite place for anglers of trout. To the west of these lay the watermeadows, used for watercress, also grown in the shallow parts of the Wye in Wycombe Marsh, Loudwater and Wooburn.

When Lord le Despencer made his diversion of the Oxford-London Road about the middle of the 18th century, the new road crossed meadowland running parallel with the river until it joined the Old Watery Lane where it turned off at Oakridge Road. The completion of the road was marked by the Pedestal, made by Banister Watts, a local stonemason, in 1752. In the Newland area, a small amount of building had taken place with cottages going up in Newlands and Loakes Lane. But essentially Newlands was meadowland with hedge-rows and trees. Newland Bridge was in a bad condition in 1728, for at that time the old timber bridge was replaced by a brick one.

The High Street was described by Browne Willis as 'a spacious well built street' and he estimated the number of houses in the town as about 300. The High Street proper started at the Hogmarket on the north side, and Crown Lane on the south, as the area to its west, containing the Guildhall, was considered to be the Cornmarket. Crown Lane was previously known as Maidenhead Lane from the Maidenhead Inn which it originally contained, but earlier it was known as Alley's or Haly's Lane, and was called after the family of that name.

The Antelope inn was the centre of military activity in the town in the 18th century, for Wycombe from the 17th century was of strategic value, due to its relationship to main roads and the Thames. The prison in Frogmore was a home for 'maimed soldiers' whose upkeep was met with funds received from the King's Bench and the Marshalsea Prison. In the 18th century it was common for a regiment to stay in the town for a considerable time.

It was in such circumstances that the poet Samuel Taylor Coleridge spent some months in Wycombe. When in 1793 he got into debt, he joined the 15th Elliot's Light Dragoons, serving in the ranks from December 1793 to April 1794. He was quartered in a public house which stood at the bottom of Easton Street called The Two Brewers, but as his educational ability became known to one of the officers, due to Coleridge writing a Latin tag on the wall of the stables, in April 1794 he was discharged. In the summer of 1794 there was a crack cavalry regiment quartered in the town under General Gwynne, a favourite of George III, which was in a state of near mutiny due to cruel treatment meted out by order of Major Shadwell. One trooper, having been mercilessly flogged twice in one day, committed suicide. Major Shadwell who was more than once mobbed for this cruelty while at Wycombe, was shot by a deserter at Maidstone.

The guard room was opposite the Black Boy, which originally stood on the corner of Noyce Lane, a row of gabled cottages which stood next to the churchyard and which was demolished in the 1930s to enable Church Street to be widened. In the 1770s the military guardhouse was at the Antelope. This building was the site of the Royal Military College. It was Lieut Col Gaspard Le Marchant's brainchild and was intended as a college along the lines of the Royal Military Academy at Woolwich, but with technical training suitable for staff officers. Le Marchant moved to High Wycombe and took over the Antelope which was 'an old place, but it will do to begin with' and with General Jarry decided to start voluntary classes for young officers. The College was officially opened on 4 January 1799. The post of Commandant went to General Jarry, General William Harcourt acted as Governor, and Le Marchant became Lieut Governor of the College. In 1801 a Parliamentary grant of £30,000 was voted and Le Marchant received the substantial salary of £2,000 per annum. A letter was sent in December 1798 to all interested parties, suggesting that they recommend suitable candidates for a place. Limited to thirty, they would pay £20 and provide their own books and instruments 'and as much of his instruction will be given actually in the field, it is very desirable that each officer should be provided with a horse, for which Forage will be allowed: General Jarry speaks very little English, therefore his lectures will be given in the French Language'.

The establishment was known as the Royal Military College with one department at Wycombe for senior officers, and another at Marlow.

In 1811 Lieut Col Le Marchant was promoted to Major Gereral and so had to vacate his position and embark for service in the Peninsular War. He was succeeded by Col James Butler, and General Jarry, who had resigned in 1806, died a year later, to be followed by Major Douglas as Inspector General of Instruction. Both had lived in the town, Le Marchant in a house in Church Street which became the Free Library, now the Wycombe Fayre Arcade. General Jarry had taken up residence in Wellesbourne House, later called The Priory on the corner of Priory Road and Castle Street.

The academic training undertaken at the Royal Military College was most successful, and is believed to have strongly influenced the Peninsular Campaign, as almost half the staff officers served the Duke of Wellington. Le Marchant died at Salamanca on 22 July 1812, after cutting down six of the enemy. Early in 1813 the Senior Department of the College moved to Farnham in Surrey.

Y having been gracioufly pleafed to accept the Offer made
, (who was for many Years at the Head of the ECOLE MILI-
N,) to take on himfelf the Superintendance of a fimilar
this Country, the Commander in Chief has been pleafed to
ollowing Particulars relative to the propofed Plan fhould
to all Colonels and Commanding Officers of Regiments,
they may recommend for his Royal Highnefs's Approbation,
e defirous of profiting by General JARRY's Inftructions, and
rictly to comply with the Rules and Regulations which
ramed by his Royal Highnefs's Direction for their Conduct,
der General JARRY's Superintendance.

will, on the 10th of March, be eftablifhed at HIGH WY-
ounty of BUCKS, and be ready to receive fuch Pupils as
Royal Highnefs's Approbation, and Leave of Abfence
ents for that Purpofe. The Number will be limited to
whom, on his Admiffion, muft pay into the Hands of
REENWOOD, Treafurers for the Eftablifhment, the Sum of
independent of which he muft be prepared to provide
Books and Inftruments, as General JARRY may think

much   be given actually in the
                 provided with a Horfe,
                 very little Englifh

                          effion is indif-
                          General JARRY
                          ho is a Candi-
                          ly grounded in
                                      the

telope Inn in High Street with soldiers on guard, 1772.
VE: The original prospectus issued in 1798 to invite students
itary College, and BELOW: Gen Sir Howard Douglas, who
r General of Instruction at the Royal Military College in
Lt General Le Marchant, first Governor of the College.

The presence of the officers brought a great deal of activity to the town, but their high spirits were not appreciated. For while Smith of White Hart Street reckoned to sell half a sack of oats each week for forage to the College and was happy to erect a notice 'Purveyor of oats to the Army' outside his house, the farmer who was thrown into the Wye as a prank was not so forbearing. There were balls in the Guildhall, and in the New Theatre in St Mary Street which was in action in 1803, plays were performed under military patronage by actors of the Windsor Company.

It would be wrong to date the entertainment and night life of Wycombe from so late a time as the 18th century. In the books of expenses of Henry VIII several companies are mentioned, attached to various towns of which Wycombe was one. In the Church is a memorial stone which reminds us that 'Near this place lies the body of Ferdinando Norton, gent., formerly one of His Majesty's band of Musicians, and many years an inhabitant of this Borough, died 1773'. A few years later, in 1795 the residents flocked to the Town Hall (now the Guildhall) to see the famous Monsieur Boaz, a conjurer whose magic amazed the town.

Another entertainment was bull-baiting. It was arranged close to the Falcon Inn at first, then carried on at the New Inn which was formerly in the West Wycombe Road. Much more leisurely was the game of bowls; in 1686 the Borough Keeper of the Bowling Green was John Sharpe whose love of nature caused him to plant a yew tree in the churchyard and leave instructions that he 'hath desired when hee Dyes to be Buryed under it'. Two years later the house and brewery in High Street known as the White House were conveyed to Thomas Oliffe, and at that time the garden ran northwards to 'Castle Hill or a place there called the Lower Bowling Alley'.

Someone else who was digging in 1729 was well rewarded as Thomas Burt, a labourer, was grubbing in Carey's Grove overlooking the town, when he discovered a sum of money, which he used to set himself up as a maltster in the High Street. The place where the money was found is now called Tom Burt's Hill, but the money did not bring good luck to all the family, for his son hung himself in the barn opposite Castle Hill in the yard belonging to Vicarage Farm. Not far from the Vicarage, just across the graveyard, were the wine vaults of Leadbeater's (now the Grapes public house).

Like most market towns, Wycombe has always had many inns, of which several are of ancient origin. The Red Lion in the High Street (now Woolworths) is old, but its site is much older, as it was held in 1482 by Robert Cok, whose kinfolk John Cokkes or Cox gave the Inn to Brasenose College, Oxford. The Antelope, which stood in the High Street, was erected about 1480 on the site of two earlier inns called the New Inn and the Saracen's Head. In 1623 the number of ale taverns in the town was reduced from twenty-one to nine, and in 1636 these included the Lyon, the Nagshead and the Katherine Wheel. In 1790 the British Directory listed twenty-four inns, besides numerous other victuallers, wine and brandy merchants, and maltsters. The way in which the ale was supped and the wine tasted was described vividly by Thomas Phillibrown on his visit to Wycombe in October 1758. 'After supper ye glass circulated cheerfully and Mr Mayor toasted His Majesty and Royal Family which was pledged by ye whole company. After drinking, chatting and a song or two from Messrs Pharsonage and Medwin (who attended with frequent intervals of solemn silence, according to ye custom of Englishmen) about half past ten Mr Mayor and the rest of ye gents took their leave and went home except Messrs Zach, Allnutt, Alder, Clarke, ye drunken clergyman, Hill the Surgeon and Pharsonage ye Attorney. They stayed to finish ye wine left on ye table and my landlord Mr Brickwell came to help but he was drunk before dinner and was now scarce able to walk. About half past eleven, my brother gave us ye slip and went to bed. As ye glass circulated, My Landlord and the parson grew so enfeebled that they could scarce fill their glasses. About half past twelve ye parson was forced to walk off and with great difficulty could get out of the door. About quarter past twelve we all broke up. Zach and Allnutt and Pharsonage in good spirits, Hill with difficulty could walk in a strait line. Callamy and self in good sober order, but my Landlord Brickwell we left dead drunken in his chair.'

West Wycombe Park - a view of the cascade.

ABOVE: The Royal Bucks Hussar, c 1890, with Lieut Coningsby Disraeli MP, and BELOW: the Bucks Militia (3rd Battalion Oxford and Bucks Light Infantry) on parade, 1908.

Roads and Robbers

The expansion of High Wycombe over the years has not only involved the building of new roads, but also changes of both name and direction of the older ones. Domesday Book notes that there are 'horses for the court', so cartage was requisitioned from time to time from the manor, and in 1170 following such a demand, waggons were brought from Wycombe to take the Kings's Household plate to London from Woodstock. When Henry II was building his new Palace there, the road from London through Windsor and Wycombe was in use and both John and Henry III also used it. The old road was called Watery Lane. It ran into Wycombe south of the river from Oxford (roughly on the site of Desborough Road) and crossed the Marlow Road, ran on in front of Loakes House as the Old Windsor Road, and followed the foothills on its way through Wooburn to the Thames near Windsor. By the 18th century this old road had lost some of its traffic, but enough existed for Daniel Defoe to include Wycombe in the maltmaking towns upon the Thames. Thomas Oliffe of the White House in High Street sent as many as 1,500 sacks of malt a year between 1732 and 1739 to Queenhithe from Taplow. On their journey back, the barges would bring iron, coal and groceries, unloading at Hedsor and Spade Oak Wharves.

Despite this route to the capital, some traffic from London by 1676 entered the town via Beaconsfield and through 'a descent beset with woods' via Loudwater and Wycombe Marsh. In March 1681 Parliament was opened at Oxford, and the road was so full of coaches 'that there was going down Stokenchurch Hill fourteen coaches and I believe thirty horse at one time'. Carrier carts ran regularly on Wednesday in 1700 from the George at Aldersgate and the Saracen's Head in Friday Street for Wycombe, and by 1790, the Shrewsbury Mail-Coach 'goes through this town on its way to London every morning about three or four o' clock; and returns about twelve o'clock at night; the Birmingham Post-Coach passes through...stops at the Red Lion Inn in this town every day to breakfast about nine o'clock in the evening to the Antelope Inn; the Worcester Coach breakfasts going up at the Three Tunns, every day at eight o'clock (Thursday excepted); returns every evening at five o'clock to the Antelope, fare 7s' and other coaches included the Gloucester Coach and the Oxford Coach, while 'William Dancer's waggon goes to London every Monday and Thursday'.

In 1671 Widow Stonehill and John Fosset of Oxford started a one-day stage running from Oxford to London every Tuesday, Thursday and Saturday, and back on the odd days 'performed if God permits' but it was not God but the Vice-Chancellor of the University who stopped it and a notice was posted 'this coach was sentenced by the Vice chanc...because it was set up without my leave'.

The road was handed over to the Turnpike Trust following a petition in January 1718 describing the section from Stokenchurch to Enslow Bridge as ruinous and dangerous in winter, and later the section from Beaconsfield to Stokenchurch 'is now become so ruinous and out-of-repair that in the winter season it is dangerous to travellers'. So in December 1718 a Bill was placed before Parliament for the establishment of a Beaconsfield-Stokenchurch Turnpike Trust. This trust collected tolls by 1724 and this enabled Lord Shelburne to close the Old Windsor Road and bury part of it under the ornamental lake in the grounds he had enclosed, known today as The Dyke. In order to clear the bottleneck in front of the old Grammar School in Easton Street, it was agreed in 1767 to pull down part of the School front, including the south transept of the 12th century building.

From Wycombe to West Wycombe the other new road was made in a straight line by Sir Francis Dashwood using chalk from the caves. The original toll houses were built along the roads entering Wycombe, one in London Road opposite the Trinity Chapel, replaced in 1826 at a cost of £500 by the one which, until recently, backed on to the Cricket Ground further along the road, but which was recently demolished and now moved for use in the Chiltern Open Air Museum.

In 1768 attempts were made to extend Crendon Lane northwards over Wycombe Heath. Until then the top of Crendon Lane had been closed by a gate and beyond it was only Townfield and the ancient hollow way which led to the Heath. But the Turnpike Trustees now planned a road from Hatfield via Amersham, Wycombe, Great Marlow and Henley to Reading, with the first meeting of the Trustees taking place at the Red Lion. Toll houses for this road have also gone, but one stood on the site of the baker's shop at Terriers and another on the opposite side of the town, at the crossroads now called The Turnpike at Booker. It was told of this road that it had been built to make the journey easier for Lord Salisbury to travel from Hatfield to Bath to take the waters.

The London-Oxford toll road became more important and an Act was passed in 1823 which revised the powers of the Trustees and laid down the tolls: for horse drawing coaches 6d; for horse or beast drawing waggons with wheels 6 inches in width 6d; horses unladen 2d; oxen, cows 10d a score; calves, hogs, sheep, pigs 5d a score. The value of the tolls in 1837 was in the region of £3,500 at which figure they were let — ten times greater than the value in 1724. But in 1848 Henry Kingston wrote 'much of the prosperity of the town has declined in consequence of the almost total suspension which railway transit has given to the activity and excitement of the hourly influx of coaches and posting'. For Wycombe had been by-passed as the new railway ran from London to Oxford. In an attempt to remedy this oversight, in 1847 Royal assent was given to the Wycombe Railway Bill to connect the town with the Great Western Railway by a branch line from Maidenhead, and for many years Wycombe was the railhead town for the surrounding district. The line was extended to Thame in August 1862, and further extended to Oxford on 24 November 1864. During August 1870 the lines from Wycombe were closed to allow the conversion of the rail to standard gauge, and the Wycombe Railway Company was absorbed by the GWR in 1867. November 1904 saw a large force of men shift the downline platform of the new station, to accommodate the doubling of the line. During the construction of the Whitehouse Tunnel in 1902 between Loudwater and Beaconsfield, six men were killed as the roof fell, but despite this, the new line was opened in 1906 — a joint venture between the Great Western and the Great Central Railway — to give Wycombe a direct line to Marylebone.

Accidents happened on roads as well as rail, for in 1779 a baker was crushed to death in Frogmore as the Bicester stage lurched too close to the houses as it sped through. More dangerous were the risks of highwaymen and robbers on the main roads around Wycombe. In 1227 a merchant from Fairford was murdered in Robert Glorie's wood at Wooburn. The roads were so bad that they were only fit for heavy traffic in the summer.

The toll bars which were put up to stop passage of non-payers were most unpopular, but as coaches became greater in numbers, so the roads were made more useable and so the risk of robbery became greater. The London-Oxford Road was a favourite hunting ground for highwaymen and coaches were often attacked as they laboured up Dashwood Hill. Dick Turpin is believed to have patrolled the Oxford Road.

A much more local highwayman was Jack Shrimpton of Penn. Jack Shrimpton 'used to commit his depredations upon almost every Coach and Horseman between London and Oxford, and once near Stokenchurch robbed a Barrister of fifty guineas and stole his horse.' But he was captured in London, convicted of murder and five robberies on the highway and executed in 1713.

A murder which caused most consternation in High Wycombe was that of Mr Pontifax on 2 January 1736. Thomas Phillibrown visited the site in 1758: 'Miss Brickwell showed us at a distance ye field where honest Mr Pontefrac, a farmer was shot many years since by two rogues who dodged him from ye late Mrs Haydon's, our customer at ye Antelope at High Wycombe to who he was related by marriage and at whose house he had been to receive money and came down ye Antelope about 12 at night, from whence ye rogues dodged him and in a field about a mile out of ye town towards West Wickham on ye right hand of ye West Wickham Road, they first shot Mr Pontefrac and then robbed him. They pretended to ask him ye way to West Wickham and while he was going to put them on ye right road, they commited the foregoing cruel murder. Mr Pontifax had only his son with him, a lad about 12 or 13 years old who immediately when he saw his father shot, ran and alarmed the townspeople of High Wickham who came up and found the dead body.' The two murderers were both taken in the Rag Fair at London and were tried at Aylesbury Assizes. The story is taken up by the *Northampton Mercury* of 22 March 1736. 'This morning early, Marsh and Marshall, condemned for the murder and robbery of Mr

Pontifix the farmer, near High Wycombe, was brought in a cart from Aylesbury, to Rye Common, and about Eleven o'clock were executed on Gibbet of an extraordinary height, being twenty-eight feet high, that the spectators who were very numerous, might have the satisfaction of seeing justice done on two villains, who had deprived of life a person highly esteemed by all that knew him.' On this occasion the crowd was so great that the front wall of the Royal Grammar School was pushed over by the press of people trying to get to the spectacle. The bodies were left hanging for about four years before being cut down, and the cross pieces of the gibbet were eventually taken down and used as the top rail of the bridge which crossed the stream into St Mary Street.

In the early days of the 19th century policing was in the hands of a Town Watch. The constables were only on duty at night or during fairdays and elections, and their duty was to see to the closing of the inns, to place in prison drunkards or strangers wandering around the town after dark, and finally to ring the Town Hall bell at any outbreak of fire, or if reinforcements were needed to apprehend criminals. The prison or House of Correction as it was then called, was in Frogmore, and it was established under the Charter of Cromwell, to replace the old gaol under the Guildhall. It was probably on the north side of Frogmore, on a site subsequently demolished to make way for the Palace Cinema. The prison was built in 1659 and it had a Governor or Keeper; the earliest recorded one was Thomas Fisher, who held the position until his death in 1686. It was not a pleasant place, for when a group of Quakers were imprisoned there in 1665, they termed it a loathsome dungeon. A new gaol was built in the Police Station which was erected in Newlands in 1816-7, and which was in use until 1936 when the present Police Station in Queen Victoria Road was built. The Governor also appointed two night watchmen, later increased to three, and they covered the three beats of the town, namely High Street, St Paul's Row and Frogmore, 11pm to 6am. The Watch House stood next to the Church, in the churchyard, and when it was leased to Mary Allen in 1697, the deed provided that 'in case souldiers shalbe quarted within this Borrough that they shall have liberty to watch and keep gard in the sd Watch House'.

Following the Municipal Corporations Act of 1835, the Borough Council created a Watch Committee, who on 3 February 1836 appointed James Cooper and William Venables as Night Constables at a weekly wage of 10s 6d. They patrolled from 10 30pm to 4.30am and on Saturdays and Sundays 8pm to 3am, taking the beat alternatively. After winter, the Borough economised by changing the duty from 11pm to 4am at a lesser weekly wage of 8s until Michaelmas. On 6 February 1839 the Watch Committee appointed the Beadle and Town Crier George Davis as Superintendent of Police, a position he served for forty years. The uniform was a suit of police clothes, a hat with silver braid, two pairs of shoes and he had a salary of £15 per annum, rent free house, and fees for 'crying goods' in the market. The Lock-up was under the Great Market House, and there were frequent reports as to its filthy condition.

The police force was re-organised in 1849 with two full-time officers in addition to the Superintendent, and following the 1856 County and Borough Police Act wages were increased to 16s per week. The Chepping Wycombe Extension Act was passed in 1880 and by 1882 the force had been increased to ten, and officially reported 'practically efficient'. Its size grew to 19 by 1901 and in 1947 when powers were removed from the Borough, it stood at a Chief Constable and forty-five men.

The real test for the Wycombe Police Force came at the General Election of 1910, which was based on Free Trade against Tariff Reform. As part of the publicity a 'Dump Shop' which exhibited items imported into England duty free instead of providing work for English workers, was opened in the town. After the result of the poll, when Sir Alfred Cripps was elected 'unprecedented scenes of disorder in the town' began on the Friday afternoon and crowds assembled on Saturday night, and though 'a large number of extra police had been drafted into the town…they were unable to hold the crowd in check and eventually at an early hour on Sunday morning the Mayor read the Riot Act, and baton charges were made by the police'. The Dump Shop was attacked, the contents set on fire, and the mob looted the shop; then the Conservative Club was attacked and the windows smashed.

The specials who had been sworn in were 'fighting like tigers' amongst themselves so were dismissed. After the baton attack 'it was estimated that between thirty and forty had to be medically treated'. On many of the streets the blood stains were still to be seen, and on the following Thursday a protest meeting took place at the Guildhall to complain at the reading of the Riot Act and 'the brutality of the Police toward the inhabitants of this Town'. But the answer to the charges came in April when the Mayor stated 'the streets were cleared after every opportunity had been given for the people to disperse quietly. The County police did their duty most efficiently on that occasion and undoubtedly saved the town from a great destruction of property and possibly loss of life'.

Terrier's Toll House, 1909.

ABOVE: A Cockney and his wife going to Wycombe. BELOW: The Tally Ho Coach of West Wycombe, 1929, and RIGHT: The Wycombe Coach Horn.

ABOVE: The first motor 'bus, 1908. BELOW: Borough of Chepping Wycombe Police Force Badges: LEFT: White day helmet badge. RIGHT: Black night helmet badge. ABOVE: Small white cyclists' badge.

FORM B.

FORM OF PEDLAR'S CERTIFICATE.

In pursuance of "The Pedlar's Act, 1871," I certify that *William*

Robertson of the Borough of Chepping Wycombe, in the County

of Buckingham, aged *52* years, is hereby authorised to act as a

Pedlar within the Wycombe Borough Police District, for a year from the date of this

Certificate.

Certified this *26* day of *July* A.D.,

187*6* .

Geo Davis

Superintendent of Police.

This Certificate will expire on the *25th* day of

July A.D., 187*7* .

Acc. no. 73.

ABOVE: Ankle chains used in the local gaol, and BELOW: A Pedlar's
certificate of 1876.

WYCOMBE
MUNICIPAL CORPORATION

THE COUNCIL.

Mayor. Alfred Slone Esq'r
Justice. John Turner Esq'r

Aldermen. Mr Jas G Tatem.
. Alfred Lane
. George Harman   } 9th Nov.r 1844.
. Robt Wheeler   } 9th Nov.r 1847.

Councillors Mr Thos Wheeler
. Thos Treacher
. B Jos Tuck   } 1st Nov.r 1843.
. John Young
. Joseph Hunt
. Percival Wright
. Willm Jackson   } 1st Nov.r 1844.
. Henry White
. John Turner
. John Nash
. Geo S Parker   } 1st Nov.r 1845.
. Willm Cotman.

Town Clerk. Mr John Parker
Treasurer . Mr John Harman
Auditors. Mr H. Crook, & Mr G. Harman
Auditors. Mr Wm J Butler & Mr S. Nash
Mayor's Auditor . Mr G. Wright.

Sergeant at Mace . James Day
Beadle & Cryer .   George Davis

DAY-POLICE.
George Davis .   Superintendant.

NIGHT-POLICE.
William Cooper .
William Scrubles .   } Watchmen.
George Fry .   }

CONSTABLES

John Harman .   . Frogmoor Ward .
John Davis .   . Pauls Row Ward .
N.L. Beasley .   . Frogmoor Ward .
James Shepard .   . Pauls Row Ward .
Moses Blinko .   . Easton Ward .
Thomas Wright .   . Easton Ward .

Quarterly Councils
On January 19th April 20th July 20th and
October 19th .

Wycombe Municipal Corporation: the list of Police and Night Constables, c 1847.

ABOVE: The Watch House in the Parish Churchyard, demolished c 1935.
BELOW: Newland Police Station as it was from 1817-1935.

The Dump Shop, Oxford Street.

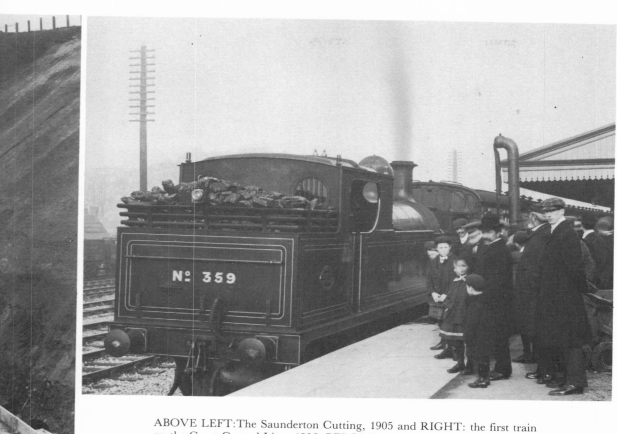

ABOVE LEFT:The Saunderton Cutting, 1905 and RIGHT: the first train on the Great Central Line, 1906. BELOW LEFT: The Wycombe Excelsoir Cyclist's Club, formed 1882. RIGHT: The King's motor car in High Wycombe c 1905.

ABOVE: The old fire engine, with BELOW: the Wycombe Volunteer Fire
Brigade on the Rye, c 1890.

ABOVE: The Volunteer Fire Brigade outside the new station in Priory
Road, 1901, and BELOW: outside the Town Hall, 1922.

107

ABOVE LEFT: One of two long service medals belonging to H.S. Wheeler, covering 35 years of service in the Volunteer Fire Brigade, and RIGHT: the Silver Plated Trophy Fire engine, complete with helmets. BELOW: Fire at the Wheat Sheaf in High Street, 1903.

The Furniture Trade

The making of furniture, (and in particular the making of the Windsor chair,) has been the staple trade of High Wycombe since the middle of the 18th century, when farm workers turned the chair parts in the surrounding woods. There is a reference to Andrew Kelsey, a tablemaker of Wycombe in 1349, and to a turner in the parish registers of the 1680s, while in 1695 John Rowell's lease of the Old Guildhall was renewed by his son for use as a joiner's shop. It was Daniel Defoe's comment in 1725 which points to a more organised approach: 'A vast quantity of Beechwood which grows more plentifully than in any other part of England' was used for making 'beech quarters for divers uses, particularly chairmaking and turnery wares'.

The earliest local reference to a Windsor chair is in the Church Records of West Wycombe for 17 December 1732, when a 'wins. chair ordered by the Vestry' was purchased, and later in the century, the list of craftsmen between the ages of 15 and 60 eligible for military service in 1798 records over fifty chairmakers in the Borough and Parish of High Wycombe and West Wycombe, without taking into account those over the age of sixty. Chair legs and other turned parts made in the woods had for some years been sent up to London and Birmingham to be made up into chairs. Later a local farmer decided to make premises available in Wycombe.

When a woodturner bought a stand or fall of trees, he would rig up his workshop within the woods. At first this would be an open hut with sloping sides meeting at the ridges and thatched with brushwood and bracken, but in later years when the tools and material were more likely to be stolen, the wood and galvanised hut made its appearance.

The term 'bodger' has been more recently applied to the chair-leg turner who makes the legs and stretcher and sticks which are used in making up the chair. The origin is uncertain and may not have been in common use until the present century, chiefly in a derogatory way. The pole-lathe, used by the chair-leg turners working in the woods, was a crude but effective piece of machinery on which a competent operator could turn out a gross of legs a day. For each four legs the bodger turned, he would also have to make a set of three stretcher parts for the underframe, so the total number of pieces in a gross soon reached 250. In the years before the Great War, he could expect to get 5s a gross, but by 1920 it had risen to 14s a gross. The pieces were taken in sacks to the factories, where the framer fitted together the various parts.

The first factories were centres where the parts of the chair were assembled together, so representing an early example of mass-production, and we find by the late 18th century that chairmakers were already advertising. The 1790s bill-head of William Treacher announced that he was a 'Windsor, dyed and fancy chair manufacturer' while James Gomme in 1798 was labelling his furniture 'Sold at the original Upholstery Warehouse of James Gomme, in High Wycombe, where cabinet work is done, and orders for household furniture of every description, in the best and most fashionable manner'. Thomas Widgington and Samuel Treacher were attributed with starting the first of the late 18th century factories, and an early apprenticeship indenture of 1809 exists between Widgington and the Trustees of Lady Jane Boy's Charity, which arranged for a poor boy to be trained in the arts of turning and rush seating. Widgington's factory, which was in St Mary Street, was destroyed by fire in 1812. Daniel Glenister was apprenticed to Samuel Treacher, and the firm of Thomas Glenister was established in 1839 and is still active in the town, its premises in Temple End. Another early manufacturer was Walter Skull and a pattern book of the firm, dated c1849, is in the Wycombe Chair Museum.

Between the years 1800 and 1860 the number of factories grew to fifty. In 1830, it was estimated that there were '200 persons employ'd in the industry and a chair produced a minute throughout the year [over one million chairs a year]'. By 1870 the town was producing an estimated 5,000 chairs a day. Large contracts were taken; in 1873 Glenister's received an order for 19,300 chairs for the Moody and Sanky evangelical meetings, which was completed in a few weeks and despatched to London. Glenisters employed 250 men. Similarly the town supplied 8,000 chairs for Crystal Palace, and in 1874 Walter Skull made 4,000 rush-seated chairs for St Paul's cathedral at four shillings each. Later, in 1907 tenders were requested by the War Office for 30,000 chairs for barrack rooms and married quarters.

Many of the smaller assembly shops were established behind inns, the landlords of which purchased the turned items from the bodger to be made up by workmen on the premises. This proximity to the bar was somewhat of a curse, and it was a sad indictment of the times that a mother could complain that her husband and their 12 year old son could both come tottering home drunk on Saturday, having drunk a good part of both their wages.

Chairmaking firms such as Hutchinson's, Birch's, Jane's, North's and Glenister's began to make quality furniture. The attitude of the workmen was summed up in later years by Charles Skull: 'in many cases they were unable to alter their methods of work they were not used to'. The Chairmakers' Protection Society was formed in 1855, and by 1872 The Chairmakers' Trade Union provided an official 'List of prices' for work completed by workmen, broken down into more than two hundred and fifty separate and individually priced jobs.

By the middle of the 19th century a different picture emerges. Significant was the chair submitted to the Great Exhibition of 1851 sponsored by Prince Albert. This chair, designed by Edmund Hutchison of High Wycombe, won the title of 'The

Champion Chair' and was an example of the elaborate carving popular at that time. Town pride in its civic chairs soon became mandatory. In 1869 Edwin Skull, a Chairman and Town Councillor, presented the Corporation with a 'handsome chair intended for the seat of the Mayor' but in 1877, another Mayor, Cllr G. Wheeler, presented another chair as 'he found from presiding at a public meeting how uncomfortable the chairman's seat was'!

Mechanisation came in the mid 19th century and steam power saw mills largely replace the early sawpits, Plumridge's Saw Mills starting in 1866. In 1874 there were fifty chairmakers in the town with an annual turnover of £250,000. In 1885, competition came with the popular Austrian bentwood chair, produced by Michael Thonet, but Wycombe firms met this by adopting more machinery, and two firms, Glenister and Birch, answered the challenge by themselves making bentwood chairs. The number of chair factories in Wycombe in 1889 was between 120-130, and by 1895 about 150 employed 5,000 hands with the bulk of the Wycombe trade still in cane and rush-seated chairs. The close relationship between Lord Carington and HRH Edward Prince of Wales was the reason for several Royal visits to the town, and in 1884 the Prince and Princess of Wales agreed to accept a gift of two Wycombe chairs. On most occasions that Royalty was expected, arches across the roads would be erected, with pride of place going to the Chair Manufacturers' arch at the Guildhall. Queen Victoria on her visit of 1877, stopped to admire it, so when the time came for the Golden Jubilee in 1887, it was a popular idea to present the Queen with a chair from the children of the town.

The caning girls who seated the chair frames made in the factories worked either at home, taking the chair seats to the cottage to work on, or they were employed directly in the factories. Starting work at the age of eleven or twelve, it might be three years before they finished learning their trade and could earn good money on 'good best' canework. The piece rate in 1900 was 2¾d for a caned seat, with rushed seats at 6d.

The firm of Frederick Parker (now Parker-Knoll) had much experience of making fine reproduction furniture, so they were commissioned to produce eighty Chippendale style chairs to furnish the liner 'The Ophir' in which the Duke of York (later George V) sailed around the Dominions in 1901. This was near the time of the accession of Edward VII, and the Wycombe firm of Thomas Glenister supplied a number of chairs and stools for the Coronation Ceremony in 1902. The task of supplying the chairs at the Coronation of George VI in 1937 and Queen Elizabeth in 1953 fell to the firm of William Hands & Son. More recently, W. Davies & Co, which specialises in dining chairs, completed an order for 72 chairs for the Investiture Room at Buckingham Palace. While several furniture firms in the town have participated in orders connected directly or indirectly with Royalty, the provision of a continuous supply to the Crown has been the privilege of G.H. & S. Keen for over fifty years. The original Royal Warrant was granted to Sidney Keen by George V in 1925, and in 1955 his son, George Keen, was granted the Royal Warrant by Queen Elizabeth II, and his son, Mr Peter Keen of William S. Toms Ltd, followed in the family tradition by receiving the Royal Warrant of Queen Elizabeth the Queen Mother for Bedding Manufacture.

For many years the cottage industry existed alongside the factory system, with the wood turner still making the legs and stretchers in the woods and the women working on the caning and rushing of chair seats in the home. With the introduction of machinery, production soared and local industry extended the product range to include the designs of the 18th century masters. The firm of Birch, at the turn of the century included many designs in the then modern Art Nouveau style.

During the First World War (1914-18) chair manufacturers made such items as wooden rifles for the training of Kitchener's Army, gunwheel parts, struts and propellers for aircraft — tasks similar to those undertaken during the Second World War. Designs towards the end of the 1939-45 War and immediately after were strongly influenced by 'Utility' standards and later, styles changed dramatically. Chairmakers such as Gomme designed the G-Plan system — a range of matched pieces. Ercol did much to re-vitalise the Windsor Chair.

At the same time traditional furniture is still made, while in the field of upholstery and fireside chairs, Parker-Knoll have held an important place in the industry since the 19th century. Once again machinery had been modernised; steam engines gave way to electricity and now computer tapes and electronic devices help to guide modern machinery. The furniture industry has brought work to linked industries, especially in fabrics and upholstery materials with firms such as Parker Tex and Non-Sag. The expertise of Richard Graefe Ltd in the field of marquetry has enriched furniture and other panelling since the company was established in 1837. The manufacture of the machines used in the industry has been made by such Wycombe companies as Rye Engineering for many years, and no less than seventeen subsidiary industries have flourished here.

The tradition of producing impeccable civic furniture has continued, and recently two ceremonial chairs were presented to the Worshipful Company of Furniture Makers by the late Lucian R. Ercolani, Chairman of Ercol Furniture in 1972. Made of elm they 'represent thought and work over twenty years' and the panels on the back of the Master's chair contain montages of the basic tools of the furniture maker carved in bas-relief.

The woodturner's camp, c 1865.

ABOVE: The workmen of John William's chair factory at Desborough Park Road, 1901, and BELOW: inside the machine shop in 1900, showing the young lads at work.

ABOVE: Skull's factory, c 1870, and BELOW: Walter Skull that same year.

The badge of the High Wycombe and District Furniture Manufacturers' Association.

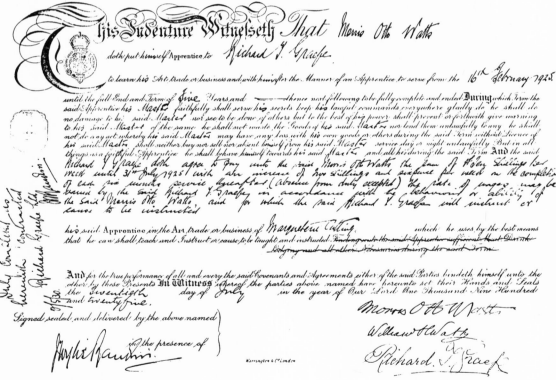

ABOVE: William Treacher's bill heading of the 1770s. BELOW: The indenture of Morris O. Watts, apprenticed to R.T. Graefe in 1925 to learn the art of a marqueterie cutter.

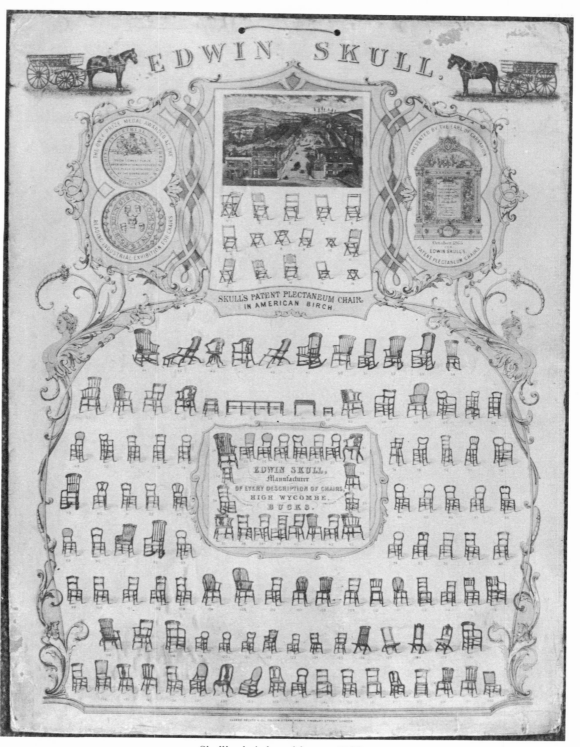

Skull's chair broadsheet, c 1866.

ABOVE LEFT: Harry Towerton's cart bringing rushes into Wycombe, c 1880, and RIGHT: caning chairs at the cottage door, with BELOW: Glenister's loaded up waggon, ready to take chairs out of Wycombe, c 1870.

ABOVE: First steam lorry loaded with 700 chairs, 1903. BELOW: First traction engine removing timber from railway to Plumridge Saw Mills; LEFT: Champion chair of 1951, designed by Edmund Hutchinson, and RIGHT: Master's chair of 1972 designed by Lucian R. Ercolani.

Chair arches erected for ABO
to see Disraeli, and in honour
Australia in 1890 in CENT
Crendon Lane. CENTRE:
honour of Prince Edward's
Mary Street to welcome Lor
the Boer War in 1901, with
and Dragon, West Wycon
Dashwood back from New
railway station t

120

isit of Queen Victoria in 1877
ord and Lady Carington from
and BELOW: at the top of
at the Guildhall in 1880 in
GHT: The arch erected in St
Bucks Yeomanry home from
ch erected outside the George
99, to welcome Sir Edwin
ELOW: the archway at the
troops in 1901.

ABOVE: Portrait group of Daniel Clarke, C.W. Raffety and J.G. Peace.
BELOW LEFT: The 'Muffin Man', J. Herbert, and RIGHT: the return of
the Bucks Volunteers from the Boer War, 1901.

122

Enterprising Expansion

The Wycombe tradition of 'Children, Chapels and Chairs' truly came to life in the nineteenth century, when the town, with a population of 2,349 in 1801 grew by the extension of its boundaries, by an influx of industry and increased commercial success to 17,683 in 1901. In 1833 Commissioners examined the various smaller boroughs, and in December 1833 they held an inquiry at Wycombe. The Corporation was included in the second class of small boroughs, and they found it sufficiently prosperous, though 'not likely to increase in prosperity to any great extent'. The Commissioners recommended that the borough should be divided into wards for the election of Councillors. The Corporation was reduced to four Aldermen and twelve councillors, out of whom the Mayor was to be chosen.

This became law on 7 September 1835, and it revoked all sections of the Charters with which it was in conflict. It swept away the old Burgesses, the right of holding Quarter Sessions and the right to appoint a Coroner and Recorder. The allowances for the Mayor were also abolished, and all charities in the hands of the Corporation were placed in the control of a Board of Trustees. As to the size of the borough, they recommended that 'We shall therefore only propose such an extension of the present Boundary as will be sufficient to compromise the whole of the Town, and any probable increase that may be made to it'. In fact there was little change.

In 1849, the Public Health Act was passed, and the Council soon found itself with problems. There were many open cesspools in the town, of which the River Wye was often considered the worst. The Borough Council also felt that to apply provisions of the Act in the field of sanitation would be to involve the town in ruinous expenditure. However in April 1849 they reluctantly received a visit from T.W. Rammell, a Board of Health Inspector, who insisted on an enquiry in view of the drainage, and mortality rate which ran at twenty three thousand. The Borough resisted, but Dr William Rose, who was Mayor and also Medical Officer of Health was in favour. Early in June, Thomas Rammell arrived to conduct the inquiry, and immediately received an antagonistic response from Charles Harman, Solicitor, one of the Committee who acted for the Borough. Every device was used to delay the inquiry; witnesses who had originally agreed to attend court could not be found, and in two instances, specific charges of intimidation were produced against Joseph Hunt, a Town Councillor, and an ardent Methodist. The findings of the report tell of the graveyard so full of graves that bones were dug up when digging a new one, and of thirty two people in Bridgewater Yard (off St Mary Street) using one privy between them.

Although the 1833 Commissioners foresaw little expansion of the Borough, Newland Meadows was partly built over for the working class of the town. Around this area and beyond Newland, the built-up area stretched beyond the formal boundaries of the Borough with houses going up along Hughenden Valley as far as Temple Hill (now the Beaconsfield Arms site) and along the West Wycombe Road to the Bird-in-Hand. Newlands itself was part of the Frogmore Ward which was divided by the river into two parts, the one called Frogmore, and the other called Newland. Some of the meadow strips remained from mediaeval farming, but for the most part, it was covered with rows of small cottages and houses with 'courts' and 'yards', communal water supply and privy and the inevitable public house on each corner. Before 1850 Newland had become a small self-contained community with shops and Leadbetter's Brewery near the river. Gas was laid on in 1850; Mendy Street, Union Street and West End Road came into existence in the early 1870s and shortly after this the old Watery Lane, formerly known as St John's Lane, became more respectfully called Desborough Road.

Perhaps the most significant change in the town came in the 1860s and 1870s when the new prosperity and the growing demand for better houses made itself felt. Town houses were built along the lower Oxford Road, Temple End and Temple Street, and permission was obtained from Parliament in 1876 for All Hallows Lane to be extended past the Vicarage through part of the churchyard to create the modern Castle Street and so link up with the top of Crendon Lane. Along London Road and on the lower part of Amersham Hill some higher class houses were built, and there were clusters of houses at Terriers, Marsh Green, Loudwater and Sands which formed the nucleus of the small villages which eventually became amalgamated with the town. In 1843/1844 the Little Market House and the Guildhall were repaired at a cost of £191 5s 0d, in spite of a petition demanding the removal of the Guildhall as it was considered a hazard to traffic. To avoid such problems the poultry market was moved from High Street to Church Square in 1824, and in 1810 the streets in the centre had been paved with Denner Hill Stone.

Among those active in the improvement of Wycombe was Mr Vernon, who tried unsuccessfully in 1872 to get the Council to install a good drainage system, and he was also rebuffed when he tried to introduce a water supply, although a little later in 1875 the High Wycombe Water Company was formed. His chief efforts were directed towards the extension of the Borough boundaries, which were finally agreed in 1880. He was elected Mayor in 1883, 1884, 1892 and in 1889 was the first Chairman of the newly formed Chamber of Commerce. Pride in the Borough in the 1870 caused J.O. Griffits QC, Recorder of Reading, to persuade the Borough Council to sell the centre of Frogmore to him for re-development. Mr Griffits laid out the open space with York stone, erected a stone drinking fountain, also a large basin with a powerful fountain jet in the centre and several jets around the outside. The fine elms were retained and the square was officially opened in April 1877. As part of the growing interest in education in the Borough, in particular with industrial growth in mind, the Technical and Arts School was erected in Frogmore in 1893. When the old Grammar School in Easton Street was vacated in 1919, most of the departments of the Technical School went there. In old photographs of Frogmore the small cottage-like building at the point of the gardens was the Engine House where the fire-engine, formerly kept in the Church Porch was located; the Engine House was built in 1861. Although the Fire Brigade was not established until 1868, two fire engines were in existence in 1860, but they were in bad condition. Following a meeting in 1868, the Fire Brigade was formed and a new engine was purchased in 1887. The charge for calling both fire engines was seven guineas, and when only one was used five guineas were charged, excluding cost of horse and driver. A new station was built in Priory Road in 1899. In 1938 George Thomas Miles was awarded a certificate for long service covering fifty two years, and J. Abbott, a founder member, served the Brigade from 1868 to 1906. The High Wycombe Fire Brigade remained in existence as a Borough Fire Service until 1941.

The chapels were beginning to make inroads into the traditional Church of England preserves. The Union Baptist chapel went up in 1845 from designs of Octavius Jorden in Easton Street, only to be burnt down in 1908 and rebuilt shortly afterwards to designs of Thomas Thurlow. The Primitive Methodists commenced their worship in a loft down a gateway in Easton Street, and now had the new building in White Hart Street built in 1875 to designs of Arthur Vernon. The Wesleyans had their chapel in a yard in St Mary Street which was transferred to the new building in Priory Road, opened in 1875, while the congregation at Trinity Chapel, which originally met in an ancient loft called 'Old Ebenezer' came to their chapel in 1850 overlooking Pann Mill, and the Salvation Army started their new Hall in Frogmore in April 1909.

The Society of Friends still worshiped in their chapel in Crendon Lane, and a little further down on the opposite side of the road was Christchurch, built in 1889-97, designed by Arthur Vernon, but like the other buildings in this street, demolished during the rebuilding of the 1930s. The Sunday School spirit was strong in the town, and the Sunday School Treats were an important part of the social life of the community. Of interest was the work of Henry Keen in West Wycombe Road, who in 1852 called into his cottage the boys from the streets to form a Sunday School Class. He raised funds and in due course built the Bird-in-Hand Sunday School in 1859.

If the conscience of the town was in its Sunday Schools, then the heart of Wycombe was in its local elections, which raised many a local councillor to apoplexy and exposed many a sitting candidate to ridicule. In the centre of the campaigns were the supporters of the Abbey and of the Borough with families such as the Raffetys, Steevens, Thurlows and Wheelers caught up in the action. Their broadsheets and other political leaflets show clearly the outspoken comments of the 1870s against which the almost unemotional campaign methods of the 1970s pale into insignificance.

Few candidates nowadays would, I suspect go as far as 'John Blunt' in October 1874: 'It is the Abbey against the Town, a struggle for life and liberty. Men of

Wycombe be worthy of your fathers! be true to the great principle of local independence they fought for...Respectable artisans of Wycombe! steady mechanics! sober fellow-townsmen! Shall your Mace stand behind the bar of a Ginshop? God forbid!'.

Soon after the 1874 local elections, the run-up to the new borough changes started, which resulted in the Chepping Wycombe Extension Act of 1880. The four old wards of the 1835 extension were abolished and the Borough enlarged to include the built up parts of the town, then redivided into three wards. It had an area of 676 acres and a population of 10,000 persons. The new Corporation consisted of six councillors from each of the three wards, six Aldermen, and the Mayor was chosen from these.

In April 1897 Lord Carington offered the Corporation a site in Castle Street for a new Town Hall in the garden of the Red Lion, as part of the celebration of the Diamond Jubilee, but this offer was not taken up until some six or seven years later when the site was switched to Queen Victoria Road. The Wycombe Cottage Hospital was opened in 1875 and a new wing called the Disraeli Wing was opened in December 1891 by Coningsby Disraeli.

War was only a short while away, and in December 1899 the call up of reservists of the 1st Battalion of the Oxfordshire Regiment for the Boer War was announced with 130-140 local men leaving on their way to the Depot at Oxford. In May 1901 the Boer War, ended with the troops returning from South Africa, and they were given a great welcome at the Railway Station in High Wycombe.

St Mary Street Sunday School outing of the 1890s.

ABOVE: The Cottage Hospital, Priory Road, in 1890. BELOW: Castle Hill House.

LOST!

The following articles are supposed to have been lost in certain parts of the Borough on the Evening of Monday, November 2nd, 1874, or early on the following Tuesday morning :---

1.—Two unfinished Councillors' Gowns, one without the sleeves, and the other without skirts, marked in tailor's chalk J.W. and R.S.

2.—Ward's "majority," a somewhat slippery article, and resembling in character a "Will o' the wisp," but with the slight difference that it is visible only in the morning and usually disappears about four o'clock.

3.—Spicer's ditto, (a similar article).

4.—Wootton's ditto, a very minute particle, resembling in size a homœopathic globule, but black as a "Smith." (A doubt has been expressed as to the actual existence of this article, so that too close a search need not be made for it.)

5.—The Brass Band, used at great political victories; supposed to have been overcome by excitement in a preliminary rehearsal of the "Conquering Hero."

6.—A quantity of torches, marked *G. M. Young, maker, Wycombe*, intended to have been used in a triumphal procession, headed by Messrs. Westrup, Phillips, Cockram, Briden, Darvill, &c., &c., but which, from unavoidable circumstances, was indefinitely postponed.

7.—A "Globe," with a face of brass, and marked L. Rolls about with a great noise, but is known to be hollow, and only dangerous to people of weak intellect.

8.—A Councillor's Gown, re-made and entirely re-lined in November, 1873, but since much stained and otherwise damaged, marked W.V.B., Loakes.

9.—A rusty Key of the Municipal Borough, labelled "Wycombe Abbey," dropped in front of the Town Hall about four o'clock on Monday afternoon.

Any person bringing either of the above articles to the Crier will be rewarded out of the funds generously placed at his disposal for charitable purposes by Messrs. Ward and Spicer, the future Aldermen of the Borough.

P.S. No. 9 was picked up by Mr. Justice Wheeler when in company with Councillors Thurlow and Raffety, and taken at once to the Mayor, who, in thanking them, expressed his decided opinion that no person was entitled to have such a Key in his possession; that the *proper* Key was held by him in trust for the people, and he hoped that the Burgesses would take great care not to send anybody to the Council Board who was likely to take a wax impression, either for the Abbey or Loakes. The Borough would not tolerate any tampering with its Independence.

November 3rd, 1874,

An 1874 Local Election poster.

ABOVE: The bonfire on Tom Burts Hill in 1897, with INSET: 1887 Jubilee medals. BELOW: St Mary Street, c 1890.

ABOVE: West Wycombe Park. BELOW: The opening of Frogmore, 1887, with INSET: J.O. Griffits in 1870.

ABOVE: High Street in 1859, drawn and published by John S. Austin.
BELOW: Dames' School, Newlands, c 1875.

ABOVE: Frogmore c 1900, showing the School of Art and Technology and the earlier site of the Salvation Army. BELOW LEFT: Miss Lines, who kept a school for young ladies in Frogmore, c 1830. RIGHT: West Wycombe church.

ABOVE: The corner of Priory Road and Church Street c 1890, and
BELOW: McIlroys on the corner of Priory Road.

ABOVE: Building
Queen Victoria Road,
1901. BELOW
LEFT: Dame Frances
Dove, the first woman
Councillor, in
procession, 1907, and
RIGHT: the new
Corporation Street in
1902, with Davenport
Vernon's on the
corner.

The New Century

Following the end of the Boer War and the death of Queen Victoria, the Borough was involved in yet another Extension Act, and in 1901 its size rose to 1,620 acres and its population to 17,683, with the make-up of the Council again altered to allow for four wards, each electing six councillors, the councillors electing eight aldermen.

In 1907 the first motor omnibus started in High Wycombe, introduced by Mr Putman from Thame. The earlier horse 'buses, used since 1892, were commenced by Llewelyn Weston, a carriage builder, and ran from the town to the Swan at West Wycombe in one direction, and from the town to the White Blackbird at Loudwater at 3d a trip each way out of High Wycombe. Mr Weston sold his interest in the business to the Livery and Posting Company and the horse 'bus continued until 1912 when the Livery and Posting Company went over to motor 'buses. They soon lost their monopoly and the London and General Omnibus Company took over as the chief transport concern. The supplier of private motor transport at that time was Davenport Vernon and Co, whose business had started as R.D. Vernon & Co, ironmongers, at the corner of High Street and Crendon Lane. He then moved to 15 High Street where he built the Central Hall, supplied bicycles, tricycles and had a smithy and wheelwrights' shops at 34 High Street. This venture into motor transport was linked with the new premises in Corporation Street (now Fads) where the Wycombe Motor Cycling Club, started in 1904, was centred. In time Davenport Vernon provided taxi cabs, distributed Rover Cars and increased the repair facilities of the business, forming the basis for the firm's present activities further down London Road at Wycombe Marsh.

A matter for concern was the decision of the War Office to disband the Bucks Militia in 1908. Their headquarters had been in Wycombe for some years, and the colours had been presented by the Duchess of Buckingham at Wycombe Abbey Grounds in May 1869. The Colours were handed to the Vicar of High Wycombe for safe-keeping on 1 July 1908.

By October 1914 Belgian refugees had begun to arrive, and in December over 2,000 troops came from Halton, and the Girls' High School was requisitioned as a hospital. Following the tradition of heroism which has won several Victoria Crosses for men of Bucks, 2nd Lieut Youens, of a Wycombe family, who was in the Durham Light Infantry, won this highest award for throwing live enemy bombs out of the gunposition in which he and other troops were in action. The second bomb exploded in his hand, and he died of his wounds two days later. During the war the town lost more than one hundred men, and another hundred at the end of the hostilities were prisoners of war or missing. In memory of these, the Memorial Hospital was built, opening in 1923.

The Palace Cinema opened in 1909, opposite its present site, then the Electroscope, later called the Rex, opened in 1912, and the Grand in 1913 in Desborough Road. The Majestic came in 1926 to be renamed the Odeon. Frogmore was the location of Aleck Stacey's covered heated swimming baths, which he built in 1910 on the site of the old Wycombe Steam Saw Mills at the Dovecote. Another open air pool opened in 1911 behind the cattle market. The bath on the Dyke was opened in 1911, another heated bath opened by Cllr Stacey in the Old Technical School in Frogmore in 1929 and in 1924 another was built at Desborough Recreation Ground which survived to 1947, and the new open air heated pool was built on the Rye, opening in 1957.

Between the Wars the character of the town changed; no longer was furniture-making the sole trade, and an influx of workers diffused the traditional nature of the population. Yet still many family firms survived. Hull Loosely and Pierce started as separate firms in the 1860s, supplying clothes, acting as builders and undertakers. Butler's started in 1906 and grew into today's large furniture business in Gordon Road. Raffety's has continued through four generations for over a hundred and twenty years, and when Reginald Rivett opened his first shop in 1923, he little envisaged the present Murray's into which it has developed.

Although the 1920s and 1930s saw changes in the industrial scene, many names that were prominent in the 19th century, such as Gomme, Birch, Castle, Bartlett, Goodearl, Skull, Hutchison, Glenister, Parker, Hands, Howland, Cartwright, Dancer & Hearns, were still playing a prominent part. The supply of timber was still arranged by such as Jonathan Plumridge Ltd, Smeaton Hanscombe and Co Ltd, Bambergers Ltd, while the popularity of rubber and plastic moulded units introduced firms like Lintafoam Industries Ltd, Harold Baker Ltd, Vita Foam Ltd, and Non-Sag Seating Co. More particularly the growth in engineering has been a feature in the 20th century, and while only 550 were engaged in this industry in 1929, the total engineering labour force in 1955 had risen to 5,600. Broom & Wade has been a leading firm, formed in 1898 by Harry S. Broom, and the original staff of twelve grew to something in the region of 1400. Older still was Dexter & Co of Queens Road, founded in 1880, making woodworking machinery. Other names include Ernest Turner (Electrical Instruments) Ltd and J.W. Cubbage & Son which was established in 1881, making steam and hotwater plants, and oil firing plants.

This change in the range of activities saw the arrival of Harrisons & Sons Ltd, in 1933, who make stamps for all countries of the world; research and manufacture of pharmaceuticals represented by G.D. Searle & Co Ltd, and R.H.M. (Rank Hovis MacDougal). To house these, new industrial estates opened up at Cressex following the 1934 extension of the boundary, with factories built there in 1937, and at Sands, Wycombe Marsh and the back of London Road. New industries require housing, and the 1920s and 1930s found the development of council estates at Desborough Road from 1926, Bowerdean from 1925, and Castlefield from 1939, and the number of inhabited houses in the borough shot up from 4,664 in 1921 to 10,215 in 1939. The Hatter's Lane Farm area was the first housing project after the 2nd World War, when a contract for 82 houses in 1946 was started, and between 1947 and 1971 the number of houses again increased, from 10,864 to 18,775 within the boundaries of the borough.

To meet the demand for water, two reservoirs had been built at the junction of Shrubbery Road and Amersham Hill, and another further up the Hill, and these, with the water tower from which Tower Street in Terriers takes its name, served the town up to 1932. A new bore hole was sunk at Pann Mill in 1910, and a 2 million gallon reservoir built at Bowerdean. The open spaces in the town were well used and these were increased with the acquisition of Holymead in 1934, part of Hughenden Park in 1936, and Tom Burt's Hill in 1937. In 1923 the Governors of Wycombe Almshouses Charity handed the control of the Rye to the Borough and the 1927 Act reduced the rights of the inhabitants in relation to it. In order that the public should not lose all their rights of access, it was agreed that the use of the mead should be limited to 10 acres and for a period not exceeding 24 days in total in the year, so enabling the Wycombe Show and other events to go ahead.

The Borough Extension of 1928 took the Borough from 1,620 acres to 4,385 acres, and the population to the region of 29,000, but only a few years later they were seeking still wider boundaries. In the end they accepted an extension in 1934 which increased the Borough to 7,091 acres, and the population to about 40,000. The new parts included Cressex, the village of West Wycombe, including Chorley Road and Pictonville and part of Hughenden and part of Downley. Much of West Wycombe had been purchased in 1929 by the Royal Society of Arts and preserved as a 'fine picture of English Life and History'. In 1934 the Royal Society handed the property over to the National Trust, and a short while later, Sir John Dashwood gave 59 acres of land on Church Hill, and a final act of generosity took place in 1943 when Sir Francis Dashwood transferred West Wycombe House and Park to the National Trust.

The civic buildings of the town date also from the inter-wars period, with the Municipal Offices in Queen Victoria Road opening in 1932, the Public Library in 1932, the Police Station in 1935 and the Post Office, which moved from Easton Street, in 1934. New schools were built with the large new secondary modern school at Mill End opening in 1937 to cover the whole borough, joined by Hatter's Lane in 1940. While new buildings had come, many had gone. The Council had been buying properties in Crendon Lane and in 1937 started demolition to widen the street. Church Street was straightened by the demolition of the Black Boy, and Noyce Alley which ran along the side of the Churchyard was removed, as were some of the slums of Newlands in the 1930s.

Wycombe Wanderers have, over the years, represented the spirit of the Borough in many people's view, and in April 1931, when they went to Highbury for the final of the Amateur Cup, they carried the enthusiasm of the town with them, an enthusiasm

ABOVE · LEFT: Major and Mrs Coningsby Disraeli, 1911. CENTRE
ABOVE: the Wycombe Lock-out band in 1914, and BELOW: the Town
Hall from the River Wye, 1904. RIGHT: London Road, 1902. BELOW
LEFT: Local Defence Volunteers, May 1916. CENTRE: Lily's Walk, off St
Mary Street, c 1920, and RIGHT: the Palace, 1920.

which overflowed on to the streets when the news of their 1-0 victory came through to the *Free Press* Office. The winning team was met at the station and were cheered for their success. In similar manner Wycombe Wanderers drew with 1st Division Middlesborough in the 3rd round Cup-tie in 1974-75, though Wanderers lost the replay.

If Wycombe had changed between the wars, those changes were nothing to what followed in post-war years. Hitherto the town seemed to consist of four Wycombes, the Easton Street side, like a village street leading to the Rye, the busy town centre of High Street and Queen Square; the attractive cottages and houses of St Mary Street and Lily's Walk, and the down-to-earth community of Newlands. The changes of the 1960s saw the disappearance of Newlands completely, and most of St Mary Street and of Lily's Walk; Easton Street has been robbed of many of its buildings, and the centre of the town is overshadowed by the bland modernity of the Octagon.

In the world of politics, the Liberal T.A. Herbert was elected in 1906, only to be unseated by the Conservative Sir Alfred Cripps in the explosive election in 1910, and during the following thirty five years the constituency returned Conservative Members of Parliament right up to 1946 when Winston Churchill went to the country. In his campaign, the wartime leader visited High Wycombe, standing, as did Disraeli 114 years earlier, next to the lion on the portico of the Red Lion Hotel, but the Labour candidate John Haire was returned. The Conservatives regained power in 1951, and Wycombe elected the Hon W.W. Astor, who was soon to go to the House of Lords, so the town returned John Hall, who acted as their Member of Parliament for over twenty-five years, was knighted, known and respected in the parliamentary division until his sudden death recently, quietly followed by Lady Hall's death in 1978. In the recent bye-election, the Conservative candidate Ray Whitney was returned.

The 1970s has been a critical decade, for it saw also the demise of the Borough of High Wycombe, when the local government re-organisation took effect in April 1974, amalgamating the Borough with the Wycombe Rural District and the Marlow Urban District into the new Wycombe District Council. Among the last civic events of the Borough was the granting of the Freedom of the Borough to Royal Air Force Wycombe in 1971. This honour has been received by a select number over the past hundred years, notable amongst which have been the three members of the Raffety family, Charles W. Raffety, F.W. Raffety and Percy Charles Raffety. Others included Roland Clarke, Bob Darby, John K. Taylor and Geoff Baker, and similar honours have gone to Lieut General Ira C. Eaker, 1st Commander of the 8th US Air Force, Sir Arthur Travers, Commander of the British Bomber Command, Colonel Lewis Clayton Reynolds, and to the Royal Green Jackets.

Seven centuries link Roger Outred, our first known Mayor, with the Town Mayor of today, and many of the traditions and customs of the town have survived the ravages of time. In 1977 we looked back twenty-five years to see the changes which had taken place, and now we must look forward once again to preserve that heritage.

ABOVE: High Street looking up Crendon Lane, 1922, with BELOW:
Crendon Lane, demolished c 1939.

ABOVE: The Municipal Offices, opened 1932, with INSET: the Industry Week
token. BELOW LEFT: The Freedom Casket given to the Green   Jackets,
and RIGHT: the Jubilee Chair made by William Hands and Son, 1977.
CENTRE: Sir John and Lady Hall.

The Dovecot multi-storey car park.

Bibliography

Ashford, L. J.   *The history of the Borough of High Wycombe from its origin to 1880.* 1960.

Ashford, L. J. & Haworth, C. M.   *The history of the Royal Grammar School High Wycombe 1562 to 1962.* 1962.

Berry, G.   *The origins of Sandhurst. Bucks Life* (Jan 1969) pp.35-6.

Berry, G.   *The token issuers of Wycombe : a study of 17th century Chepping Wycombe. Bucks Life* (Sept 1967) pp.16-18.

Berry, G. & Morley, P.   *A revised survey of the 17th century tokens of Bucks. Numismatic Jnl* (1973) pp. 96-125.

Bowerman, E.   *Stands there a school: memories of Dame Frances Dove.* 1965.

Bryant, T. H.   *Notes on the manors of High Wycombe.* (photocopy at High Wycombe Central Library).

Bucks Free Press.   *Bucks past and present.* Suplement Feb. 1979.

Bucks Free Press.   *1856-1956 : Centenary Supplement.* 1956.

Clare, R.   *The history of lacemaking : How to make lace; Lacemaker's equipment.* three articles *Bucks Life* Apl-June 1969.

Colmer, F.   *(Series of articles on the History of High Wycombe printed in the Bucks Free Press in the 1920s-1930s)*

Colmer, F.   *Records of Battle of Wycombe Rye. Bucks Free Press* (29th Nov. 1935)

Coppock, J. T.   *The Chilterns : description of Ordnance Survey one-inch-sheet 159.* 1962.

Directories (various directories exist which cover High Wycombe from the late 18th century to date - photocopies and originals of which are in the High Wycombe Central Library; Aylesbury Central Library and Bucks Record Office)

Escott, B. E.   *History of the Royal Air Force, High Wycombe.* 1970.

Escott, B. E.   *A short history of West Wycombe.* typescript. High Wycombe Central Library.

Goodchild, W. W.   *The economic development of High Wycombe.* 1933 typescript. High Wycombe Central Library.

Green, H.   *A century of education in South-West Buckinghamshire.* 1970.

Green, H.   *The parish church of High Wycombe: The Fabric and history. The interior and social background.* 2 vols 1964, 1966.

Green, H.   *Village life in the 18th century.* 1976. (W. Wycombe)

Green, H. E.   *From a Buckinghamshire Town and other poems and prose.* 1977.

A guide to the Church of St. Lawrence, West Wycombe. 1974.

Hartley, B. R.   *A Romano-British Villa at High Wycombe. Records of Bucks vol.16* (1959) pp.227-257.

Hayden, J.   *Facts and Figures : a brief historical account of Trinity Chapel, High Wycombe.* 1855.

Head, J. F.   *Early man in South Buckinghamshire.* 1955.

High Wycombe Society.   *The Rye, High Wycombe.* 1976.

Howland, P.   *A history of the Wycombe Borough Police Force 1836-1913.* typescript. High Wycombe Central Library.

Hussey, C.   *Bassetsbury Manor. Country Life* Sept 30th 1933 pp.338-342)

Jackson-Stops, G.   *The West Wycombe landscapes. Country Life,* (June 20,27, 1974)

Kingston, H.   *The history of Wycombe.* 1848.

Ledger Book of the Corporation of Chepping Wycombe: First Ledger Book, transcribed by R. W. Greaves. 1956. *Second Ledger Book 1684-1770* transcribed by W. A. Newall. 1965.

Lipscombe, G.   *History and antiquities of the County of Buckingham.* 1847. *vol.3.*

McQuaid, I.   *Miss Hannah Ball, a lady of High Wycombe.* 1964.

Mayes, L. J.   *The History of Chairmaking in High Wycombe.* 1964

Mayes, L. J.   *The History of The Borough of High Wycombe from 1880 to the present day* 1960

Mayes, L. J.   *The Wycombe Paper Riots. Paper Maker* (1964) pp.68-73.

Oxfordshire Record Society.   *Journal of Sir Samuel Luke.* 1950.

Parker, J.   *Account of the Hospital of St John the Baptist. Wycombe. Archaeologia* (1884); *Records of Bucks* vol.5 254-8.

Parker, J.   *A brief history of the Church of Christ in Connexion with Crendon Lane Meeting House in Chepping Wycombe.* 1848.

Parker, J.   *The early history and antiquities of Wycombe.* 1848.

Pevsner, N.   *Buckinghamshire.* 1960. rp.1973. *(Buildings of England series)*

Phillibrown, T.   *Diary.* (typed extracts re High Wycombe 1750-1758) High Wycombe Central Library.

Powley, P. J.   *Wycombe Marsh Union Baptist Church 1857-1957 : A century of Baptist Witness.* 1957.

Priestley, N.   *The Chepping Wycombe Borough Police Force 1836-1947.* Typescript. High Wycombe Central Library.

Rammell, T. W.   *Report to the General Board of Health on a preliminary inquiry into the sewerage, drainage and supply of water, and the sanitary conditions of the inhabitants of the Borough of Chepping Wycombe.* 1850.

Reid, K. C.   *Watermills of High Wycombe.* Chilterns Magazine (Summer 1950) pp.54-57.

Royal Commission on Historical Manuscripts.   *5th Report, pt.1 : Report and Appendix. 1876.* pp.554-565 (Borough of Chepping Wycomb.

Royal Commission on Historical Monuments.   *Inventory of the historical monuments in Bucks.* 1913. 2 vols.

Shorter, A. H.   *Paper mills in the Wye Valley.* Paper Maker (Octo 1960) pp.52__55.

Sparkes, I. G.   *The English Country chair : an illusrated history of chairs and chairmaking.* 1973. rev.ed. 1977 (based on High Wycombe industry)

Sparkes, I. G.   *High Wycombe as it was.* 1975.

Sparkes, I. G.   Royal and civic furniture. in *Silver Jubilee Memento of High Wycombe.* 1977. pp.6-11.

Sparkes, I. G.   Royal links and sovereign visits. in *Silver Jubilee Memento of High Wycombe. 1977.* pp.2-5.

Summers, W. H.   *Cromwell's Charter, High Wycombe.* Records of Bucks (1897) pp.511-528.

Summers, W. H.   *Early paper-mills in Buckinghamshire.* Records of Bucks. vol.VII

Summers, W. H.   *History of the Congregational churches in the Berks, South Oxon and South Bucks Association with notes on the earlier nonconformist history of the District.* 1905.

Summers, W. H.   *Wycombe under the Commonwealth.* Bucks Free Press 1895 (newscutting in High Wycombe Central Library)

Thoumine, R. H.   *Scientific soldier: which is a biography of General le Marchant.* Bucks Life. (Jan 1969).

Tilley, J. E.   *Industrial evolution of High Wycombe : a geographical study.* 1958/9. typescript. High Wycombe Central Library.

Victoria history of the counties of England : Buckinghamshire. 4 vols. 1901.

Index

Numbers in *italics* refer to illustrations

146

Subscribers

Presentation copies

1 The Mayor's Parlour, The Town of High Wycombe
2 The Chairman's Parlour, Wycombe District Council
3 Buckinghamshire County Council
4 High Wycombe Central Library
5 High Wycombe Chair Museum
6. Clive Birch

7 Ivan Sparkes
8 Joan & Tony Lammiman
9 M.J. Leslie
10 Valerie M. de Newton
11 Edward F. Harman
12 Mrs J. Tully
13 C.M.D. Knox
14 Miss L. Parish
15 Bernard J. Clifton
16 A. Leach
17 D. Church
18 R.D. Menday
19 R. O'Connor
20 Robert Powton
21 Phyllis Joy Willson
22 Wellesbourne Adult Education Centre
23 Carol Bates
24 John Alfred Heather
25 Alan James Kenny
26 Mr & Mrs Bernard Peatey
27 Mrs Patricia A. Taylor
28 David Bernard Audcent
29 G. V. Worley
30 A.J. Worley
31 A.J. O'Neill
32 Mrs J.S. Spencer
33 Marion Miller
34 C.T. Smith
35 Mr & Mrs I.D. Stone
36 Peter Chard
37 Mrs C.P. Clanfield
38 P.F. Farmborough
39 M. Bailey
40 I.F. White
41 Ursula & Hanns-Peter Schneider
42 Stephen Siderfin
43 Robert W.A. Barber
44 A. Conway
45 Mrs P.A. Chamberlen
46 A.G. Curtis
47 Mrs Kaye Mawdesley
48 L. Brill
49 Douglas Grange Mealing
50 Karen Sarah Harwood

51 Ric Ives
52 Mrs J.E. Shorter
53 G.A. Collins
54 Mrs D.M. Clarke
55 Miss J. Long
56 Mrs V.J. Beadle
57 B.C. Summerfield
58 Miss T.E.V. Vernon
60
61 John Leslie Gerald Felix
62 D.A. Rudd
63 E.R. Clark
64 B.B. Howland
65 L.S. Jackson
66 Mrs M.J. D'Silva
67 V.T.G. Heather
68 Miss P.D. Ridgley
69 A. Phillips
70 Mrs S.B. Hemsworth
71 C.G. Wilkinson
72 Mrs S.N. Wilkinson
73 Mrs Valerie Cowdery
74 Gerald A. Becket
75 D.J. Woods
76 Mr & Mrs R. Flint
77 Mr & Mrs M.E. Keys
78 Mr & Mrs L. Rolls
79 Mr & Mrs D.J. Barker
80 Barry George Howell
81 Mr & Mrs J. Graham
82 Marian Buckley
83 Vernon Francis Power
84 Mrs V. Colclough
85 Mrs S.A. Bridge
86 Mr & Mrs A.J. Hetherington
87 Mrs K.D. Stevens
88 G.F. Hourihan
89 William George Williams
90 Mr & Mrs D. Richards
91 J.W.H. Holmes
92 Mrs G.A. Davies
93 Mrs G.A. Leach
94 Brian Minett
95 John L. Brandler
96 Jonathon E. Bailey

97 D.P. Troutt
98 G.T. Smith
99 Hugh Harrison
100 Eric J. Heath
101 Winifred B. Wheeler
102 Mrs A.M. Evans
103 K.C. Nixon
104 Mrs J.R. Willmot
105 F.G. Webb
106 Peter Dryland
107 Eric Douglas Britnell
108 Roy E. Barton
109 Derek M. Elwin
110 John Tatton Westerman
111 John Albert Harris
112 Miss K.N.I. Kearley
113 G.W. Barlow
114 F.E. Willmot
115 Pamela Gray
116 Nigel J. Wright
117 Miss Josephine McCloy
118 Walter Millington
119 D. Godfrey
120 Edward Taylor
121 Edward A.T. Bellworthy
122 Malcolm Walker
123 Miss L.M. Hancock
124 Lowndes County Secondary School
125 T.M. Shaddock
126 John T. Shipley
127 G.R. Dewey
128 A.H. Harris
129 R.F. Gray
130 Miss J.P. Lee
131 W. Cariven
132 Miss P.J. Kemp
133 E. Coles
134 Mrs Patricia Archer
135 R.E. Collins
136 Mrs Judith Goddard
137 L.J. Sears
138 F.W. Watson
139 E. Payne
140 A.R. Harris
141 Mrs B. Newton
142 Mrs D. Newell
143 Mrs V. Greene

144 Miss E.M. Jordan
145 Mrs E. Wilkinson
146 I.S. Horwood
147 J.I. Dowdall
148 Michael & Roswitha Pedler
149 A.V. Lemming
150 L. Haynes
151 B. Youens
152 P.A. Todd
153 L. Strand
154 D.O. Salmon
155 Mrs N.M. Mullett
156 Miss P. McAfee
157 Mrs S. Carr
158 Mr & Mrs D. Gibson
159 Barry P. Sutcliffe
160 Mr & Mrs G.J. Hall
161 C.A. Killingley
162 Mrs M. Harrow
163 Mrs E. McDonald
164 Anthony Briggs
165 Miss M.E. Gregory
166 P.A. & J.W. Hewett
167 H. Bridgman
168 R.V. Tilling
169 Stephen Stern
170 Esme Hadfield
171 Mrs M. Wharton
172 T.R. Sims
173 P.J. Miller
174 Michael Page
175 Timothy Clarke
176 Derek Perry
177 H.G. Stevenson
178 Gwynn Roberts
179 John Warner
180 Anthony H. Child
181 Ronald & Pamela Wilde
182 R. N. Smith
183 Kevin A. Saunders
184 Mrs A.M. Hitchman
185 Colin Robert Brand
186 Cliff Hawes
187 Godstowe School
188 Mrs D.M. Mumford
189 Mrs H. Ricketts
190 Mrs B.A. Evans

191	Marian Buckley	251	K.F. Wright	308	Mrs P. Mudge	365	Electric Installations
192	Alfred Henry Buckley	252	Mrs J. Deighton	309	Mr & Mrs E.F.J. Smith		(HW)Ltd
193	W.J. Chapman	253	Peter Jackson	310	Mrs D. Yates	366	Ercol Furniture Ltd
194	J.J.G. Lisley	254	Mrs Linda Semmens	311	Mrs S.L. Stagg	367	
195	Derek J. Gurney	255	R.J. Sewell	312	Mrs Jean George	368	IRJA
196	R.J. Pells	256	Roger Ludgate	313	D.G. Scott	369	E.H. Morgan
197	Philip German	257	Yvonne Reid	314	C.M. Winter-Taylor	370	Equity and Law Life
198	Mrs J.M. Coltman	258	Mrs R. Doherty	315	Mrs M.A. Davies		Assurance Society Ltd
199	Mrs B.E. Oblein	259	R.E. Clift	316	Michael G. McCoy	371	Mrs W.L. Thomson
200	Dennis Vick	260	Mrs N. Hobbs	317	Alan & Kay Smith	372	Lt Col Lesslie K.Watson
201	Michael K.F. Caws	261	Mrs Janet Beaumont	318	J.M. Hutchinson	373	Wm Bartlett & Son Ltd
202	Cora E.B. Croxson	262	E.R. Gray	319	James Edmund Browne	374	Stuart King
203	James Cullen	263	Mrs M. Goode	320	I.S. Biggs	375	L.A.M. Hubbard
204	Ronald Fairchild	264	Mrs W. Schofield	321	Hughenden Park Estate	376	Mrs D. Rumens
205	Mrs J. Stacey	265	Mrs A.M. Gerrard		Residents Association	377	Miss T.E. Vernon
206	Mrs A.H. Batho	266	Mrs M.E. Jones	322	Mrs C. Davies	378	Finewood Products
207	Miss M. Pierson	267	Arthur William	323	Miss P.J. Paton	379	Ltd
208	A.B. Milne		Wheeler	324	Mrs E. Garland	380	Mrs M. Howland
209	Miss P.M.L. Hughes	268	Roy Taylor	325	J.T. Mander	381	Anthony D. Smith
210	Mrs Joan Webber	269	Dr & Mrs M.H.	326	Mrs M. Payne	382	Corris G. Keen
211	D. Jones		Bowker	327	N. Roberts	383	Jennifer W. Mackrill
212	R.D. Fiander	270	Mr & Mrs R.K.	328	R.D. Welling	384	Pinza Plastics Ltd
213	Mrs J.H. Hopkins		Gyselynck	329	Frank Hudson &	385	R.L. Bowerman
214	T.W. Gardiner	271	Mrs & Mrs B. Pearce		Son Ltd	386	James Barton
215	G.A. Blinko	272	Mrs D.J. Webster	330	F.R. Hinton	387	National Federation of
216	D.R.J. Pearson	273	Stanley Thomas	331	J.C. & M.P. Smith Ltd		Old Age Pensioners, High
217	Andrew Price		Birchmore	332	Minty Furniture		Wycombe
218	P.E. Lukin	274	D.G. Minns	333	George Stone	388	Harry Wheate
219	G.A. Higgins	275	Roy Edmund		(Furniture) Ltd	389	D.M. Grant-Riach
220	D. Empringham		Bashford	334	Michael G. Lacey	390	R.H.G. Herring
221	Mr & Mrs D.M.	276	Mrs V.E. Webster	335	G.R. Woolven MBE	391	Harry E. Green
	Arnold	277	J. Scruton	336	James Howland	392	R.F. York
222	P.M. Collett	278	Mrs A.D. Wadsworth	337	Smyth Engineering Ltd	393	
223	D.J. Robins	279	L. Potter	339		394	Michael F.M. Prole
224	J.W. Lindsay	280	Mr & Mrs R.F. Hester	340	G. de Thier	395	Michael J. Winston
225	J.M. Joyce	281	J. Cottrell	341	Dickens and Lance Ltd	396	E.C. Meakes
226	S.N. Gay	282	Mrs Betty Hale	342	Cecil Davies	397	Alan Powell
227	M.H. Highfield	283	Harold A. Hatt	343	W.J. Shrimpton	398	C.J. Seabright
228	Mrs H.S. Smith	284	Maurice R. Marshment	344	Mr Baynes	399	M.W. Pusey
229	C.J. Humphrys	285	Carmelo Ferdinand	345	Mrs P.J. Willson	400	Mrs K. Benson
230	Mrs A.M. Chapman		Virgil Ellul	346		401	Raymond A. Chappell
231	Mrs J.A. Bentley	286	Mrs W. Coleman	347	M.W. Edmonds	402	Antony John Wright
232	Georgina Marjory	287	Rev G.A.J. Balmer	348	R.F. Bristow	403	Peter R. Williams
	Davis	288	George Ellames	349	A.E.L. Cook	404	Florence Gertrude
233	Mrs V. Weeks	289	Anthony Peter Hockley	350	D.J. Cresswell		Dunning
234	Norman C. Dilley	290	D.F. Murray	351	E.A. Stevens	405	John Iremonger
235	Euro-Japanese	291	Mrs H. Brooks	352	K.A. Saunders	406	R.H.M. Research Ltd
	Exchange Foundation	292	J. Kerr Gibb	353	Eric Powell	407	Mrs Audrey Moring
236	W. Batts	293	Graham Haines	354	F.A. Hunt(Chairs)Ltd	408	Wellesbourne School
237	C.R. Hewer	294	John Robbins	355	Browns of West		Resource Centre
238	G.D. Forster	295	Ivor L. Beeks		Wycombe	409	Malcolm Read
239	Mrs Linda Dorman	296	J.S. Gore	356	R.F.S. Vere	410	David Read
240	P.W. Eckersall	297	M. Low	357	R.H. Robinson	411	Victoria and Albert
241	Mrs I. Evans	298	W. Page	358	H.G. Simmons & Sons		Museum
242	Mrs J. Rolfe	299	K.C. Britnell		Ltd	412	Brian Robinson, North
243	G.B. Brook	300	Robert P. Robinson	359	The Thomas Glenister		Marston
244	F.H. Wiles	301	M. Leeder		Company	413	Buckinghamshire
245	Mrs J.N. Ward	302	Gail & Tony Mason	360	B.R. Gay	442	County Library
246	Mr Willson	303	Mrs L.Y. Bowman	361		443	
247	H.R. Harford	304	I.A. North		B.Cartwright & Son Ltd	444	Michael Bird
248	Mrs E.G. Dods	305	Mrs M. Clark	363			
249	Mrs T.P. Reid	306	Mrs D. Harris	364	Dr H.J.E. Cox MB,		
250	Mrs M.M. Maun	307	Mrs B.E. Butler		MRCP,DRCOG,DCH		Remaining names unlisted

ENDPAPERS: FRONT: Map of the Borough of Chepping Wycombe in
1832. BACK: Map of the Borough of Chepping Wycombe in 1932.